RISE UP

Also by Reverend Al Sharpton

The Rejected Stone: Al Sharpton and the Path to American Leadership
Al on America
Go and Tell Pharaoh

RISE UP

CONFRONTING A COUNTRY AT THE CROSSROADS

REVEREND AL SHARPTON

HANOVER
SQUARE
PRESS

HANOVER
SQUARE
PRESS™

Recycling programs
for this product may
not exist in your area.

ISBN-13: 978-1-335-96662-9
ISBN-13: 978-1-335-66879-0 (Barnes & Noble Exclusive Edition)

Rise Up: Confronting a Country at the Crossroads

This edition published by arrangement with Harlequin Books S.A.

Library of Congress Cataloging-in-Publication Data has been applied for.

Hanover Square Press
22 Adelaide St. West, 40th Floor
Toronto, Ontario M5H 4E3, Canada
HanoverSqPress.com
BookClubbish.com

Printed in U.S.A.

I dedicate this book to my grandson, Marcus Al Sharpton-Bright. I hope that by the time he's old enough to read, America will have chosen the right path forward during this tremulous time so that he will not have to suffer, endure, nor fight the unfairness his grandfather brought to light. May he read this book to better understand the injustices of our past and not our future.

CONTENTS

Foreword

AL*RIGHT*

By Michael Eric Dyson

Martin Luther King Jr. conquered the American imagination because he was cut from the most majestic moral and ministerial cloth. Barack Obama captured the Oval Office because he was a dream candidate plucked from central casting and featured as the nation's first Black president. Jesse Jackson seized the nation by its lapels when he rose from modest Southern roots to global acclaim as a freedom fighter. And Fannie Lou Hamer shattered convention and the racial sound barrier with her earthy and eloquent demands for emancipation.

Still and all, there has never been anyone quite like Al Sharpton on the American scene. Like King, he's a preacher, but far grittier and rawer. Like Obama, he's a politician, but presidents, governors, mayors, and all the rest bow at his throne even though he never held elected office. Like Jackson, he's the brilliantly evolved product of the Black bottom, but his bottom seems more, well, bottom. And like Fannie Lou, he's got vivid vernacular, but he can make it resonate in the White House or on Harlem streets. Although it's cliché to say so, it is really true that Al Sharpton is an American original. He is a man who can, at the funeral for the martyred George Floyd, talk about how roaches flee when the light is switched on in ghetto homes, just as the light of justice makes roaches of racism scatter.

The reason Sharpton can pull it all off is because he has never stopped being himself, even as that self has matured over the years. He is an unashamed preacher, called to deliver the word at the age of four, taking as his text John 14:1—"Let not your heart be troubled: ye believe in God, believe also in me." (That verse undoubtedly gave him comfort a few years later when his heart was broken, and he plummeted from middle class to poverty when his father left his mother to start a family with Sharpton's half sister. I told you his bottom was more bottom.) If you've ever heard him preach, you can hear how he was born first in Pentecostal tongues of fire and then reborn in swirling Baptist waters of prophecy. He preached his first sermon the year I was born. He has honed his craft in churches high and low, Black and white, and beyond over the past sixty-two years. And he's been mentored by some of the best Black folk in the land.

Sharpton went out on tour with gospel great Mahalia Jackson as a youth, sat under preaching legends Bishop Frederick Douglas Washington and Dr. William Augustus Jones, was tutored by the political maverick Adam Clayton Powell Jr., nurtured by the electrifying evangelist for justice Jesse Jackson, and, perhaps most famously, he got taken underwing by the Godfather of Soul, James Brown. It is well-known by now that it was Brown who, in exchange for his support and for bringing Sharpton on tour with him, got the minister to style his hair after the famous impresario of funk. As Sharpton has combed through controversies and criticism, he has maintained a permanent allegiance to his follicular forebear.

People readily identify with Sharpton because, despite his fame, he is a Black everyman. When he first broke through as an activist, he was clothed in the tracksuit and sneakers favored by young folk in his generation. Later he was sheathed in Brooks Brothers suits and other tailored fashions. He lost significant weight when he fasted in 2001 to protest military exercises on the island of Vieques, Puerto Rico, and has since shed half a man, and with it, the unjustifiable image of a racial arsonist, to become the most well-respected leader of his generation. Sharpton is arguably the last great figure of a dying breed of charismatic Christian leaders thrust into a prominence he has maintained for decades. Along the way, he was youth director for the presidential campaign of Shirley Chisholm, youth director for the New York City branch of Jesse Jackson's Operation Breadbasket, founder in 1971 of the National Youth Movement to raise funds for poor youth, and, twenty years later, founder of the National Action Network to increase voter education, registration, and turnout, to help the poor and to stimulate local community businesses. And he ran for president in 2004.

But it is as an on-the-ground activist who couldn't be ignored that Sharpton made his mark. When Bernhard Goetz shot four Black men on the New York City Subway in 1984, for which he was eventually cleared of all but the most minor charge, Sharpton protested in the streets the weak prosecution of the self-styled vigilante. When three Black men, including Michael Griffith, were assaulted in the Howard Beach section of Queens in 1986 by a white mob and chased onto the Belt Parkway, Griffith was struck and killed by a passing motorist. Sharpton led a protest march a week later through Howard Beach as its residents spewed race hate and epithets at the mostly Black marchers. His actions compelled New York Governor Mario Cuomo to appoint a special prosecutor in the case.

In 1989, four Black teens were violently set upon by up to thirty Italian youths in the Brooklyn neighborhood of Bensonhurst. One of them shot and killed sixteen-year-old Yusef Hawkins with a handgun. Sharpton led protest marches in the immediate aftermath of the event, again after one of the two ringleaders was acquitted of the most serious charges against him, and later after other members of the gang were given light sentences. It was before that last demonstration that Sharpton was stabbed in the chest, and when he recovered, he pleaded for mercy for his assailant when he was sentenced in court. Sharpton was involved in the Tawana Brawley controversy, where a young Black woman claimed to have been raped by six white men in Wappinger, New York, though it turned out later to be a hoax. Amid the firestorm of criticism of the civil rights leader, few pointed out then, and few have said since, that Sharpton's greatest fault may have been that he took Brawley seriously and at her word. As the motto of the #MeToo movement suggests, Sharpton believed a young Black girl making an accusation of sexual abuse. He did it long before social media hashtags and the concerted demand in the broader culture for gender justice.

It is perhaps his involvement in several high-profile cases where Sharpton has proved especially prescient about what has become the defining civil rights issue of our day: police brutality against Black folk. Among the most notable is the case of Amadou Diallo, a Black immigrant from Guinea who was shot to death by cops from the NYPD, whose unjust death Sharpton protested. (I was arrested alongside him and Reverend Jim Forbes in a protest march in 1999.) Or the Tyisha Miller case, where a Black teen was shot in her car during a health crisis as she lay in a comatose state holding a revolver on her lap, and when awakened, she was startled and clutched her gun. She was shot twenty-three times by cops who had been called to the scene by relatives to assist her.

There was also the case of West African immigrant Ousmane Zongo, who was shot by an undercover cop in Manhattan. Or the case of Sean Bell, a young Black man whose body was unjustly pumped full of lead with fifty bullets by plainclothes cops the day before his planned wedding. Or, more recently, the cases of Eric Garner and, just this year, of George Floyd, two Black men who were killed by cops as they pleaded for their lives in chilling similarity of expression: "I can't breathe." In these cases, and in many more, Sharpton has led protests and highlighted injustices. He has proved to be ahead of the curve in understanding just how fundamental such cases are to the safety and well-being of Black America. He understood early how they reveal our essential vulnerability in the face of law enforcement that is supposed to protect and serve us, and instead, in too many instances, has harmed and killed us. Thus, the greatest civil rights leader of our time has tackled the greatest civil rights issue of our time. He did it long before many others had an inkling or others gave him credit. He also did it at a time when so many dismissed police brutality as a problem for poor and working-class Black folk. Thus, Black elites and white officials were brought up short when it was clear that it was a plague for all Black folk.

Al Sharpton has risen to cultural heights and wields enormous political authority because he came from the lowest rungs of society but kept his compassion and love for the people. Although he has been a trumpet of conscience, he has not played just one song or sounded just one note. As a prophet, he brings Black evangelical believers further into a progressive political arc; he chastises white nationalists like, in my view, President Trump; he decries alternative facts; he champions women's rights; he supports LGBTQIA rights and, in fact, embraced gay marriage before the Black president he advised; he speaks and protests on behalf of immigrants; he tackles global warming, climate change, and environmental racism; and he provides a powerful model of principled activism, political resistance, and profound proclamation of the social gospel.

Al Sharpton never claimed to be the Almighty. But Reverend Al is certainly the best *Al*ternative to the *Al*ienating effect and the *Al*arming ignorance of many political leaders. While that bit of wordplay may be hokey, or goofy, or corny, there is nothing of the sort in the leadership of Al Sharpton. This man is a gift from God to the world. This book is a gift from Al Sharpton to us. Let's appreciate them both.

Introduction

WICKEDNESS IN HIGH PLACES

Throughout my life I've been called many names, some for better—activist, leader, father—and others for worse—agitator, fire-starter, con man. At heart, I'm a preacher, though I don't sermonize from a place of purity. If you're looking for the story or the perspective of a nicely sanitized, so-called clean Black man, Rhodes scholar, et cetera, I'm not your guy. I'm the guy who came up from the pile, which is why my clothes are still muddy. I didn't choose to grow up in the mud—no one does—but I understand those that did. There are far more of us than you probably think, and we're not all Black and from the ghetto: some of us are white and living in Appalachia. We're the people who have been knocked down and counted out, scandalized and ignored and yet—we're still standing. If you've never been tested, you're guessing what

God can do. But if you've tasted fire, if you've fought back the floods and still made it ashore, you know what God can do 'cause He done it for you. In the tradition of my faith, then, I open this book in the same manner I greet every morning— with prayer, specifically the first verse of Psalm 37: "Fret not thyself because of evildoers, neither be thou envious against the workers of iniquity."

As a boy preacher, I spent long hours reading and rereading the Bible, and yet it wasn't until my twenties that I gave this piece of Scripture a closer look. James Brown reintroduced me to it. Mr. Brown wasn't your typical Sunday churchgoer. (Despite being like a father to me, Mr. Brown never let me call him by his first name.) He'd rather be on stage, his name in marquee lights, or in the recording studio than in the pew. Toward the end of his life, however, when the stage lights had faded and he'd been through more than his share of ups and downs, he regularly attended church. He found solace in that psalm and would quote it often. Over the years, I've come to appreciate it, too. To my mind, it's a lesson in perseverance, of staying the path in spite of the evildoers, the haters, and the naysayers, those who demean and abuse, bringing people down rather than lifting them up. I still rise each morning to fight the good fight: to shine a light on those who build their wealth and prosperity on the backs of other people's suffering, who disregard the worth of any other human being on the basis of their race, class, gender, religion, cultural background, or sexual orientation.

But let's be real: the workers of iniquity are working overtime, and we, as a country, are being tested as never before. COVID-19 has laid bare the deepening consequences of the inequities in our society—not only are minorities and those in the lower class most likely to catch the virus and die from it but they are also the most vulnerable to a loss of income or health care as a result of quarantine and other measures. Socioeconomic inequality worsens the virus's spread. Besides this health pandemic, which is sure to have lasting effects, we're also facing a pandemic of racism and discrimination, which on May 25, 2020, culminated in the death of George Floyd, a forty-six-year-old Black man, who died in Minneapolis, Minnesota, after being handcuffed and pinned to the ground by Derek Chauvin, a white police officer. During the days of mass protests and civic unrest following Floyd's death, President Trump demonstrated our country's crisis of leadership, doubling down on a type of authoritarian command typically favored by dictators and autocrats. To think, after eight years in power with the country's first Black president, we've ushered in our own undoing, electing one of the slickest racial demagogues in modern history, a huckster real-estate-man-turned-politician who's laughing all the way to the bank.

President Trump flaunts his racism, sexism, xenophobia, and homophobia as if they were the Four Horsemen of the Apocalypse, bearing down on the very institutions of democracy itself. Much has already been said about Trump being a backlash to Barack Obama, a racialized knee-jerk reaction to a Black man overstaying his welcome in the White House. It's more like whiplash, and the very divisiveness it stirs up speaks to a serious ill in our body politic. Trump may not have come into political existence at all had it not been for the broader conditions supporting his fruition. But the soul of the country isn't defined by Donald J. Trump nor the policies of the GOP any more than one person or political party can bear that weight. We are defined by our shared principles, values, and sense of morality. Our democracy is still the greatest political system in the world, but it's one that requires constant engagement and course correction. Let there be no mistake: today, it is under attack.

Our nation stands at a crossroads, a historical turning point that's testing our moral character and endangering all we have fought to gain. Put aside the 2020 election, because this moral crisis runs deep. When we talk about a pandemic like it's the common flu, overlooking the needs of the country's most vulnerable population, we have a moral problem. When we talk about cutting Medicaid from your mama just because you don't like Obama, we have a moral problem. When we can watch armed white men shoot an unarmed Black man going for a jog on video and pretend we didn't see what we saw, we have a moral problem. We have a problem in this country with wage stagnation and income inequality. We have a problem in this country when Secretary of Education Betsy DeVos doesn't believe in public education, when public schools are called *government schools* by the Trump administration. We have a problem when Secretary of Housing and Urban Development Ben Carson, a Black man from Baltimore who worked his way through higher education to become a prominent neurosurgeon, has removed discriminatory clauses from public housing. We have a problem when corporations actively pollute the air our children breathe for profit. The Trump administration isn't deregulating Obama's legacy, it's deregulating the future of this country and selling its resources to the highest bidder. We're corroding from the inside.

In Ephesians 6:11–12, Paul the apostle says: "Put on the whole armour of God, that ye may be able to stand against the wiles of the devil. For we wrestle not against flesh and blood, but against principalities, against powers, against the rulers of the darkness of this world, against spiritual wickedness in high places." There's a reason we're to don our best God-given armor, because wickedness can be legalized, institutionalized, and weaponized in the form of xenophobic travel bans, discriminatory practices, legislation, and policies that roll back decades of advancements for civil and human rights, and so much more. Make no mistake: wickedness has reached high places if the president of the United States can unblinkingly equate neo-Nazis with counterprotesters. Such wickedness reduces us all to our lowest, most base instincts.

I honestly believe that we have arrived at a dark moment in our nation's history, a time when it's not clear where to look or who to believe, what action to take. God is testing us. Our Founding Fathers are testing us. We're testing one another. Provided we commit ourselves to the reckoning of hard truths and difficult choices, however, I believe we can withstand these tests. Why do I have such hope? Because I've seen too many people rise in the darkness.

In 1990, Nelson Mandela, newly released from his twenty-seven-year jail sentence, visited Mayor David Dinkins and other prominent Black leaders in New York City. I was fortunate enough to be included in this meeting. As I shook Mandela's hand, I couldn't help but think that for sixteen of those twenty-seven years, he wasn't allowed to touch the hand of his wife, Winnie. When she was arrested and sentenced to solitary confinement herself for sixteen months, Mandela didn't know of her sentencing until a prison guard told him. When his mother died, he asked permission to bury her. In order to do so, he was told to denounce the objectives of the ANC, the African National Congress. He said he would not, and so he missed seeing her laid to rest. He also missed the burial of his eldest son, Thembi. He missed watching his other children grow up. He endured twenty-seven years of court-ordered pain while his country and its people suffered, too.

When I met Mandela, New York City was still roiling from the trial of the Central Park Five: a group of five innocent boys—Latino and Black—charged with the assault and rape of a white jogger. The case had caused a media firestorm and had stirred up lingering racial animosities, prompting Donald Trump to take out his now-famous, one-page ad in the *New York Daily News* calling for the state to kill the boys. (In 2002, they were found innocent, and the state formally withdrew the charges.) Racial tensions were high, and I was feeling especially bitter about the state of things. I was embroiled in my own controversy and was still recovering from being stabbed while marching in Bensonhurst, Brooklyn, to protest the killing of sixteen-year-old Yusef Hawkins. It was during this backdrop of unease that I listened to Mandela explain that he never doubted South Africa would be rebuilt. He knew things would change, and he would not rest until they did. His struggle gave me a much-needed sense of perspective: change doesn't happen overnight. It takes time, vigilance, and courage to root out ugly truths.

A few years later, Reverend Wyatt Tee Walker, chief of staff for Dr. Martin Luther King Jr., asked me to be an election observer with him in South Africa. I will never forget witnessing South Africa's first free national election: lines of people—some of whom had been standing under the heat of a blistering sun for over eighteen hours—snaked the city streets. It was the first election in which all races were allowed to take part. That night in my hotel in Johannesburg, I learned that the ANC had won the election. I watched as the Afrikaners' flag was lowered in the courtyard of the hotel. In its place, the ANC flag rose against the night sky. It seemed to me that the collective cheers of South Africa were lifted up and carried high by shifting wind currents, both literal and figurative.

Later, I thought of election day in America, how Blacks and women had fought for the right to vote. Compared to the endless lines of people waiting to vote in South Africa, Americans have it easy. I remember begging people to vote in Brooklyn when I was a young organizer, and all it took was a fifteen-minute walk to the voting booth; I still have to beg people to vote today. My mother couldn't vote in the United States until she was in her thirties. This wasn't "back in the day." It wasn't that long ago that Blacks and women couldn't vote in this country. It wasn't that long ago that my mother dropped out of school to pick cotton for a living. My right to vote is dependent on the lives of those who came before me, people who fought against the injustices of second-class citizenship by legal and institutional enforcement. And I can't walk fifteen minutes out of my way to vote?

South Africa was seemingly without hope or power under the constraints of apartheid, and yet in the shadows of that darkness, Mandela died as the country's first free president. Think of where we were as a nation after the Bush adminis-tration: still reeling from 9/11 and mired in the beginnings of war. Dark days. Barack Obama, a Black man from a single-parent home, ran a political campaign on a message of hope and went on to become the country's first Black president. These aren't isolated moments. When Obama's hand touched the Bible on Inauguration Day of his second term, he reached back into history. He took the oath of office not on a single Bible but on two—one owned by Martin Luther King Jr. and the other by Abraham Lincoln, symbolically linking the progress of our past with the promise of our future. Where are we now? Where is the soul of this country?

Our moral compass is out of whack; we need to do some serious soul-searching and repair. To put it another way: we don't need a filling. We need a root canal. Both the Coro-navirus pandemic and the recent protests to address systemic police reform have illustrated a profound truth: we're more connected than we realize, our safety is interdependent, and our worth is only as good as the Golden Rule. Because we're so connected, we can't afford to live in silos. This applies to our sense of morality as much as it does to our political thinking. If we are to build a clear and just path forward, we must take a hard look at our collective failures and work to reclaim our moral conviction and core values—those ideals upon which America promised to be a shining city on a hill. While a president with sound moral judgment and a resolute ethical mind can help redirect our modern-day ills, this work will continue no matter who is in office. We must redefine what's right and what's fair, not only for the few and the powerful but also for the most vulnerable among us.

It's undeniable that in the past four years, the Trump administration has dangerously transported us to a time in this country when those who enjoyed the most power, status, and privilege—white men—did so at the expense and suffering of anyone not born white nor male. I have fought against racism and xenophobia for a long time. I think we are in as much peril now as we were when I was a kid joining Martin Luther King Jr.'s movement. The path that Trump would want us to follow is in direct opposition to the path this country has been on since, I would argue, the civil rights movement of the 1960s. Because Trump is working against the core values of liberal democracy, there's no clear plan beyond his impulsivity, his ability to placate the conservatives, and his flagrant attempts at recruitment. He brings his constituents into the fold by stoking an us-versus-them mentality and by appealing to hatred, fear, and feelings of distrust. His policies reflect this—from building a wall at our southern border to attempting to dismantle Supplemental Nutrition Assistance Program (SNAP) and Children's Health Insurance Program

(CHIP) during a pandemic to trying to repeal Obamacare with no other comprehensive insurance system in place. This is an administration built on cruelty all in the name of honoring the so-called forgotten people of America—farmers, truckers, and coal miners, the fading veneer of a version of white America that no longer exists, if it ever truly did. Where does Trump's path lead? It takes us back to an era of blatant disregard for civil and human rights. His path further exacerbates today's socioeconomic inequities.

Under Trump, the wealth tax has paved the way for private corporations and the wealthy to become even more well-off. The wealth gap is widening. The income gap between Blacks and whites is widening. The health care and educational disparities between races are astounding. No one is immune from these injustices, as Martin Luther King Jr. famously said: "Injustice anywhere is a threat to justice everywhere." We will never all be the same, but everyone—gay, straight, Jewish, Evangelical, white, Latino, Black, lower-class, and upper-class—should have equal protection under the law. The goal of following a path of civil rights and social justice is to create a more fair and just America, a place that doesn't exploit people but gives them access to health care, criminal-justice rights, and an equal-opportunity life. Trump's path guarantees none of that and shows no results for anyone except wealthy, white Americans.

Liberals too often get tangled up in the progressive-versus-moderate conversation, debating whether or not systemic change trumps addressing Americans' most basic needs. Imagine you and I are flying to Chicago from New York. It doesn't matter that you show up at the airport with a briefcase and I show up with several pieces of luggage. We're both headed in the same direction. I can ride with other people's baggage and, hopefully, you can ride with mine. If we're trying to get to the same place, it's best to work with your fellow travelers. What I can't do is get on a plane that's going in the opposite direction of where we need to go. If we agree that it's in our best interests to have a more equal and just world, and data suggests most Americans do, we can argue about the details of how to get to our final destination. What we can't do is let someone else hijack our ride; that is, work against our best interests in the name of making America great again for the select few.

In my life, I've run with both the dreamers and the schemers: people like Nelson Mandela, Martin Luther King Jr., and John Lewis are dreamers; Roger Stone, Don King, and Donald Trump are schemers. I've mingled high and low, with celebrities and everyday people alike. I've seen people go the way of the wicked, trading their moral compass for a taste of power, wealth, or status—I've even indulged in some of this behavior myself. But wickedness doesn't last. No one can tell me the names of the past two leaders of apartheid, but the world knows Nelson Mandela, a man who sat alone in a jail cell for twenty-seven years, dreaming of the day when he could bring change. Some people can list the titans of American industry, but the entire world knows the name Martin Luther King Jr., a man born to humble circumstances who rose up to shake the trees of justice. Good outruns bad but only if you stay the course.

David says in Psalm 37, "I was young and now I am old, yet I have never seen the righteous forsaken or their children begging for bread." At sixty-five years old, I've seen my share of battles. I've run for president, founded the civil rights organization the National Action Network (NAN), hosted television and radio shows, sat ringside with Donald Trump at heavyweight bouts in Atlantic City, tangled with more than my share of Republican politicians and leaders, gone on a five-city tour with Newt Gingrich tackling issues in education, and spoken with Barack Obama in what was his last sit-down television interview as president. I believe in my heart that I have a unique understanding of some of the key players in Washington, DC, and in the worlds of media and entertainment as well as those in the Black community. As such, I have a unique responsibility to call out what I see not for the sake of my own personal indulgences but to help us confront the hard decisions we face at the crossroads of our country today.

At the time I started writing this book, President Trump was busy telling his supporters at a rally in New Hampshire that the Coronavirus would be gone by April, claiming that when temperatures rose, the virus would miraculously go away. By the time I had finished writing the last chapter, the virus had claimed thousands of lives and plunged the world into economic free fall. Another epidemic—police brutality—stamped out the life of George Floyd, making his name synonymous with a massive uprising of rallies, vigils, and protests, the majority of which were peaceful. Besides Floyd's death, Breonna Taylor, a twenty-six-year-old EMT, was shot to death in her sleep by police in Louisville, Kentucky, and twenty-five-year-old Ahmaud Arbery was fatally shot by two white residents while jogging in Glenn County, Georgia. People were outraged. In the span of a few months, our collective moment of reckoning had arrived. Our hard confrontations with the truth will reverberate far beyond the publication of this book. We've already seen the global impact of these protests with the United Kingdom, Germany, Canada, Italy, New Zealand, and more showing their solidarity with the American protesters. In light of the moment we currently find ourselves, I've done my best to update the text with relevant insight. Most of the topics addressed, however, were already issues that have festered too long in our body politic.

This book is divided into eight chapters that cover everything from the origins of our democracy and its bold proposal as the American experiment to the Trump administration. Each chapter is organized around a particular theme or issue: civil rights and racism; women's rights and sexism; LGBTQ rights and homophobia and gender bias; immigration rights and xenophobia; and climate change. Included throughout are profiles of individuals, famous and everyday heroes both, who, in the face of real adversity, chose to rise, tackling some of these issues head-on. As their stories illustrate, the choices we make at the crossroads and the lessons learned can determine the rest of our lives. The last chapter is a practical guide on how you, the reader, can follow some tried-and-true, direct-action steps culled from my lifetime of activism to become an agent of change yourself. I close out the book with some words I gave at the eulogy for George Floyd and a call to action for our days ahead.

If you're looking for academic theories or wonkish facts, this isn't the book for you. This is a book for the outsiders and the outcasts, the rabble-rousers and the tree-shakers, people who don't give up when the die is cast but, instead, dig in their heels and ready themselves for the oncoming fight. This is a book for the dreamers and the doers. In the end, righteous *does* win; it takes longer than we'd like, and sometimes we may not live to see its final victory. Somehow, someway, however, I believe that right still finds a way. My heart, mind, and faith compel me to believe that. I'm determined, no matter how dark it gets, that daybreak won't catch me on the wrong side of the path. Let me show you how.

1

AMERICA:

Truths, Lies, and the Experiment

We are living in strange times. As I write this, Gwen Carr and I are on our way to Minneapolis to hold a prayer vigil in honor of George Floyd, who died after arresting police officer Derek Chauvin kept his knee on Floyd's neck for a total of eight minutes and forty-six seconds. Carr, perhaps better than most, understands the pain and suffering facing the Floyd family. Her son, Eric Garner, shared George's last words, "I can't breathe," before dying in police custody in 2014. Six years after Eric's death, I find myself confronting—once again—the violent reality of being Black in America.

At the same time, COVID-19 has ushered in a new phase of life in America, one that seemingly runs counter to our historical imperatives of being a nation of the free. Americans thrive on their sense of independence and self-righteous indignation—"No one tells *me* what to do!" "Don't tread on me!" We thrill to go out, network, and socialize, especially in large, urban cities. Now, however, most bistros, bars, and bodegas are either closed or in the process of slowly reopening. At the start of the crisis, the Havana Club shuttered its doors, and with it went my daily cigar. We're a country of extroverts forced indoors and away from one another, hibernating and stocking away food and toiletries. Missing a cigar with friends, however, is a minor inconvenience compared to the trials and tribulations of those on the front line—doctors, nurses, health care professionals, and scientists—along with the elderly, the sickly, and the homeless. We're living a real-life version of *A Tale of Two Cities*, with the pandemic radically illustrating the vulnerabilities of those people who live on the margins of society. Our fault lines—socioeconomic, political, and racial—are more exposed than ever before. I'm convinced that the deep civil unrest unhinging the country is, in part, connected to the racial disparities exposed by the crisis.

As of this writing, COVID-19 has sickened millions of people globally and claimed the lives of hundreds of thousands. These numbers are expected to grow. How well we're able to contain the effects of the virus depends on how willing we are to sacrifice our individual conveniences for the sake of saving the lives of others. At no other point in recent history has there been a more explicit crisis that calls for an unwavering national response: the independent free market and individual states won't help us. A mobilization of all our resources combined with strong leadership might. President Trump downplayed the catastrophic nature of the virus to the American people, failing the first test of leadership: trustworthiness. In not preparing for its imminent spread, he failed another: preparedness. When state governors pressed

President Trump for more medical equipment on a conference call early on in the crisis, our commander-in-chief told them, "Respirators, ventilators, all of the equipment—try getting it yourselves," pitting the states against one another and, most likely, leaving the poorer ones to fend for themselves. Our democracy is stronger than this president and his lack of leadership. Our values are baked into the founding of this country, and yet they seem to be floundering—and not just on matters surrounding COVID-19. To understand our present-day situation, we must first come to terms with where we, as a country, have been.

THESE TRUTHS

The American experiment is still young, relatively speaking. At a 1981 commencement speech at Notre Dame, Ronald Reagan said, "This experiment in man's relation to man is a few years into its third century. Saying that may make it sound quite old. But let's look at it from another viewpoint or perspective. A few years ago, someone figured out that if you could condense the entire history of life on earth into a motion picture that would run for 24 hours a day, 365 days—this idea that is the United States wouldn't appear on the screen until three and one-half seconds before midnight on December 31." Compared to other countries—Greece, China, Iran—we're the new kids on the block.

While the founding documents—the Declaration of Independence and the Constitution—were signed in 1776 and 1787 respectively, we're still in the process of their unfolding. We're an embodiment of their underlying truth and values, and as we change, their meanings do, too. We know, for example, that when the Founding Fathers wrote the Declaration of Independence—with Benjamin Franklin famously editing Thomas Jefferson's draft from "sacred & undeniable" to "self-evident" truths—they didn't consider Black males to be full men, nor did they consider women of any race to be equal. We also know that five hundred years ago, Native Americans weren't even part of the democratic conversation, except as notions of property or extermination. Our modern-day understanding of equality has since evolved in no small part because a long line of activists have kept the conversation and its issues front and center. I consider myself a part of this activist tradition. I'm motivated to question, challenge, and change America's inequalities because my love for this country is great and unyielding.

The day after 9/11, I was asked to provide words of comfort and healing for a special radio show on KISS FM. At 8:00 a.m., the radio station planned to synchronize with other stations around the country, all of which were going to broadcast the song "America the Beautiful." The version that played was performed by the great Ray Charles, a man who, having lost his eyesight as a child, couldn't see the amber waves of grain nor the purple mountain majesties of which he sang. The passion with which he delivered those words, however, left no doubt: he believed in the beauty and the spirit of America even though he couldn't witness it and knew of its historical mistreatment of Blacks and others. Most of us love this country for much the same reason: even if we haven't experienced the full benefits of what I would call American beauty—freedom, equality, and justice—we still believe that if we keep working, marching, and voting, we can make America beautiful for everyone. I said as much during my speech at the 2004 Democratic Convention in Boston. I closed that speech by saying, "Let's make America beautiful again." Maybe I should have passed out blue MABA hats.

From its inception, America has rested on three principled

truths—political equality, natural rights, and the sovereignty of the people. These truths were rooted in a deep sense of Christian morality. The audacity of the American experiment was that we, as a nation, would both judge and hold ourselves to these truths. This is what Martin Luther King Jr. was alluding to when he delivered his "I Have a Dream" speech, August 28, 1963, at the Lincoln Memorial in Washington, DC, in which he famously said that the nation would "live out the true meaning of its creed." In using the phrase *the true meaning*, Martin Luther King Jr. was appealing to our higher selves. These truths were something we had to live up to. At the time, however, Martin Luther King Jr. also had something else on his mind: forty acres and a mule.

There's a reason Martin Luther King Jr.'s March on Washington led straight to the Lincoln Memorial. The masses didn't go to the Washington Monument or to the Thomas Jefferson Memorial. Instead, Martin Luther King Jr. pleaded his case at Lincoln's feet. Why? Because after signing the Emancipation Proclamation just a hundred years prior, Lincoln had promised forty acres and a mule to each freed slave. Well, we never got the land nor the mule. Lincoln may have signed our freedom with the Emancipation Proclamation but, as Martin Luther King Jr. said in his speech, "the Negro still is not free; one hundred years later, the life of the Negro is still sadly crippled by the manacles of segregation and the chains of discrimination; one hundred years later, the Negro lives on a lonely island of poverty in the midst of a vast ocean of material prosperity; one hundred years later, the Negro is still languished in the corners of American society and finds himself in exile in his own land." People like to skip to the climax of King's soaring speech, but the truth is this: over 250,000 Black men were assembled at the Lincoln Memorial to collect on that promise. America defaulted on its promissory note. The Republican Party may have originally been the party of Lincoln and Frederick Douglass, but it was the Democratic Party that gave us the Civil Rights Act two years after King's speech. We got the Voting Rights Act under a Democrat, too, and so we've been riding that donkey as far as it could carry us ever since. We've gone from 1963 when the check to the Black community bounced to today when it's been stamped Stop Payment by the Trump administration. It's not that the so-called bank of America—its democratic heart and soul—is out of funds; it's that the people in power and in high offices don't have any intention of making good on the payment. Worse, gains like voting rights, affirmative action, and social service programs that were made during the civil rights movement of the 1960s have been weaponized by the political right to increase feelings of polarization, making it easier to roll back many core achievements.

In 2017, for example, the Department of Justice dropped the federal government's long-standing position that a Texas voter-ID law under legal challenge was intentionally racially discriminatory, despite having successfully advanced that argument in multiple federal courts. The district court subsequently rejected the position of then–Attorney General Jeff Sessions's Justice Department and concluded the law was passed with discriminatory intent. Later that same year, the Justice Department filed a brief in the Supreme Court arguing that it should be easier for states to purge registered voters from their rolls. One year later, the department sued Kentucky to force it to systematically remove the names of ineligible voters from the registration records. These purges, along with their sinister bedfellow, gerrymandering practices, are taking the country's voting rights hostage. The Trump administration is also quietly stripping away certain protections under the Civil Rights Act of 1963, reducing that landmark federal win to a Jim Crow era, state-by-state, George Wallace–type of mentality.

The operating governance has always been a fight between a collective union and states' rights. Make no mistake about it: the Trump administration is rolling back our collective union. We're headed—with regards to a woman's right to choose, voting suppression efforts, aggressive policing, and so much more—to a resurgence of state rights. As more and more federal courts are stacked with Trump appointees—two-thirds of them white males—conservative judges will send cases back to the state courts to uphold legislation that works in favor of the select few. Trump isn't just stacking the courts: his record-setting number of conservative appointments—fifty-one appellate judges to date—is changing the judicial landscape. These lifetime appointments will most likely seal the GOP's conservative agenda in the courts even as liberal ideas like paid maternity leave, government funding for child-care, and boosting the minimum wage have majority support among Americans.

If we went state by state during the civil rights movement, Jim Crow would never have ended. Slavery itself was a state-by-state decision. It's always been left to the federal government to stand up and protect people's rights. We saw this with the fight for same-sex marriage, with support growing for it slowly state by state only after it had been denied, for years, by some of the very same states that later adopted it. It took the Supreme Court and President Obama's vocal, unabashed support to fully turn the tide and ensure that same-sex couples were guaranteed equal dignity in the eyes of the law. This is why there's real danger in having a federal government and a justice department *not* fight for the things you believe in because…where do you go? You can no longer appeal to the federal government because under the Trump administration it's the antithesis of the progressive movement. The only place you can turn to change the federal government is to the polls, and the Trump administration is working hard—with voter suppression and intentionally inaccurate census counts, among other dirty tricks—to make it difficult for an already suspicious and media-whipped public to trust that voting not only works but is something worth fighting for.

I've had the firsthand opportunity to witness different types of government around the world and to meet with political leaders as varied as Nelson Mandela, Fidel Castro, Yasser Arafat, and Shimon Peres. As much as I question and protest and see contradictions in this country, I still feel that democracy is the best political experiment in the world. Listen, it's not a perfect system, and I would be the first to concede that it's prone to corruption. I'm especially sensitive to the tyranny of the majority, this idea that the majority will pursue its own interests to the detriment of the minority. The risks, however, are offset by the rewards. Democracy is still the most durable weapon against monarchies and oligarchies having complete control. Within a functional democracy, there's a check on absolute power, although Trump has pushed this notion as far as it can go, saying in a television interview with ABC News host George Stephanopoulos in June 2019, "Article II [of the Constitution] allows me to do whatever I want." Trump was speaking about whether or not he was allowed to fire Robert Mueller, the acting special counsel overseeing allegations of Russian interference in the 2016 presidential election, though his actions before and since suggest a broader interpretation of the power of the executive branch—or perhaps his more callous disregard for the legislative branch and Speaker of the House Nancy Pelosi.

The question of democracy, however, isn't about whether or not it's a perfect system. It's about our ability to fine-tune it and to elect the best possible individuals to give it meaning. It's about being able to have political redress and systems of accountability. It's a system that works because it allows for this kind of course correction. It's why we have the impeachment process. Whether or not you agree with the outcome of any particular impeachment, it's important to recognize that our democracy allows for this process in the first place; it's a political remedy built into our governance. For the most part, the American experiment has largely been a success. It's come to a serious standstill only once in its long history. But that breakdown unquestionably had lasting effects, many of which we still feel today.

AND A LIE

When the Founding Fathers wrote about these self-evident truths, they simultaneously sold the American public a lie. The ugly truth about America's beginning is that, for as great as it could be, the spirit of liberty bypassed the lives of the slaves who tended the homes and worked the fields of white families, including a majority of the Founding Fathers. It's impossible to talk about the founding of our country without addressing its original sin—slavery—and its legacy of racism, blatant or institutional. Around slavery and racism, the American experiment stutters time and time again.

The question I hear most often from white folk is, "Reverend Al, why do you make everything about race?" And the statement I most commonly hear from Black folk is, "Ain't nothing gonna change." Somewhere between those two extremes is a happy medium, but we haven't arrived there yet. There's a grave misunderstanding surrounding the legacy of suffering that the Black community has had to endure because of slavery and the issue of white guilt. Let's be real: we don't tell the stories of our hardship to make whites feel guilty. It's the lack of understanding and sensitivity about the suffering that Black families have historically had to endure—first under slavery, then under the thumb of Jim Crow, then under the knee of a police officer, all the way up to today's more institutionalized forms of racism—that still causes so much pain today. It's the fact that legislation is still being passed on the backs of our suffering.

When I was born, October 3, 1954, at ten o'clock at night, and the hospital issued my birth certificate, it read *Negro* for my race. That's not only a description, it's also a designation. With that one word, my station in life was prescribed by the color of my skin and, with it, the quality of my education, the neighborhood and kind of home I was likely to live in, and my occupation, because in this country—and in most countries around the world—you are identified by your race. A white child has a different designation and, in many cases, a European lineage. My ancestors were slaves. My great-grandfather Coleman Sharpton was owned by an ancestor of Senator Strom Thurmond, the famed South Carolina segregationist. Several years back, I visited the plantation where my family had lived, toiled, and died. In the field where my ancestors were buried, I also saw the marked tombstones of the family who had owned my family. It's more than a little unsettling to stare at a tombstone that bears your last name knowing that the man buried there isn't your family and that your surname doesn't belong to you either. I'm a Sharpton because the white family who owned my family were Sharptons; slaves weren't allowed to have last names. Our first names were also taken from us: a grown man was *boy* or *son* or worse. So, I'm shocked when people tell me all I see is race because I'm stunned that they *don't* see it. Being born Black in America is already a racial proposition. It's my skin.

It's my name. You act like my circumstances are my choosing and not the reality of being born Black in a country that still hasn't come to terms with its racism. I can't tell you stories about the *Mayflower*. I can't tell you about the ethnic stock of my European forefathers. But I can tell you what it's like to grow up in Brownsville, Brooklyn, my mother struggling to put food on the table. I can tell you what it's like to go to funeral after funeral of young Black boys killed because of the color of their skin. I can tell you what it's like to go from the streets to the suites of Manhattan and still be one of the few Black men in a corporate boardroom meeting.

When I visited that two-hundred-year-old plantation house in South Carolina, I found myself thinking, *What did my great-grandfather think while he worked the fields? Was he dreaming of a better life for the great-grandson he'd yet to meet? Was he dreaming of a Black president? Could he even imagine that possibility?* I tried to envision him, standing in the field or stooped low over the land. Near to the house was a collection of tiny stones hidden by some leaves. To anyone else, those stones meant nothing. But to me? As the Bible says, Jesus was the stone rejected by the builders who became the cornerstone. Those stones were the unmarked graves of my Founding Fathers, my family. To me, they were and are everything.

When you don't admit the moral outrage of slavery, which was based on race, or the hundred years of Jim Crow, which was also based on race, you not only deny the fundamental inequality of racism, you also abet it. To convince yourself that racial inequality isn't a crime, most people, wittingly or not, buy into a core tenet of racism: Blacks are inferior. It snowballs from there: they're animals; their leaders are crooks by definition; they're criminals; they're undeserving. If a Black person speaks up to redress racism, he is a racist himself. This is a slave-owner's mentality, meant to maintain a power dynamic where the status quo protects white privilege and keeps us from addressing the basic fact of inequality. If you relieve yourself of the burden of thinking that Blacks are inferior, how do you explain the health care discrepancies between whites and Blacks, the differences in unemployment numbers by race, the unequal incarceration rates and sentences for Blacks when they commit the same crimes as whites under identical circumstances?

What does it say about our democracy and the fact that it was built on the express and intentional exploitation of human suffering? What does it say that we are grappling with it still? According to a July 2019 Quinnipiac University national poll, 51 percent of the electorate say that Trump is a racist. The breakdown of that percentage is telling: whites, Republicans, men, white Evangelicals, and Catholics say he's not racist. Blacks, Democrats, women, and the religiously unaffiliated say he is. I have my own thoughts on the subject. Let's not forget that Donald Trump's formal entry into politics was based on birtherism—the unfounded idea that President Barack Obama was born overseas and therefore illegitimate to serve America.

At best, the suggestion of birtherism was a political play by a desperate man who consistently dabbles in conspiracy theory and who propped up these rumors to serve his own advantage. At worst, it's a well-worn racist trope, meant to awaken a deep fear of the Other; that is, anyone who doesn't conform to white America. Obama's name and skin color—the fact that he was born to a white American woman and a Black Kenyan man—are affronts to MAGA Americana. Despite Trump's claims, Barack Obama was born in Hawaii. There's been no serious or credible evidence to counter this basic fact.

Trump and I have been in several tussles over the years. I've known the man for over forty years. Sometimes we agree to disagree. Other times, as with the Central Park Five case, we dig in deep. The issue of birtherism was a distinct line in the sand. I disagreed with him deeply and called him out on *PoliticsNation*, my television show. I soon received a call from an old colleague of mine, a man who went to law school with Michael Cohen, Trump's personal attorney. Cohen relayed a message to our mutual associate, saying that Trump was upset I'd called him a racist. I clarified my position. "What he's doing is racist," I said. Cohen wanted to know if I would meet with Trump to discuss the issue.

I soon found myself riding up the glitzy elevator of Trump Towers with Michael Cohen. I'd been there count-less times before, and over the years, I'd met with Trump on several matters—everything from discussing the possi-bility of him working with Black businessmen on building a Chicago-based Trump Towers to talking about Freddy Ferrer's mayoral campaign to inviting him to NAN's 2002 ribbon-cutting ceremony. On this particular day, however, Cohen brought me into a room where Trump was showing an architectural display to a group of people, investors I sup-posed. Standing alongside these businessmen was Trump's daughter Ivanka as well as several well-dressed corporate types, who I assumed were part of the Trump Organization. Trump explained that he'd be with me in a minute, he had to wrap up this other meeting. I was escorted into another room. You never knew with Trump: did he stage the meet-ings to overlap so I could see him in his role as boss, or did he want his group of investors to see that he was meeting with me? Both possibilities could mean nothing or every-thing. I tried not to read into the situation too much, but knowing him, I couldn't shake the feeling that it was cal-culated, to what end I wasn't sure.

The walls of Trump's office are plastered with photographs and framed newspaper articles or magazine covers either featuring Trump in persona or Trump in name. I've been inside the offices of several public figures—everyone from Roger Ailes and Rupert Murdoch to Barack Obama and Jesse Jackson—and none displays photographs of themselves the way Trump does. His self-adulation is staggering and, to my mind, an indication of a deep-seated personal insecurity. I sat in the room in silence, waiting, with several photographic versions of Trump bearing down on me. Cohen, who was also in the room, seemed visibly uncomfortable. I got the distinct feeling he was concerned about how the meeting would go, not because of anything I might say but because he wanted to impress his boss for delivering me to him. Needless to say, the meeting didn't go well, with Trump loudly insisting that he wasn't a racist. I tried explaining how the birtherism movement was fundamentally racist—that it was a barefaced attempt to discredit a Black president. We went back and forth, and after about forty-five minutes we agreed to disagree. At no point did I apologize. Later, on Fox News channel's *The O'Reilly Factor*, Trump said, "Well, look, I know Al Sharpton better than I know you, and I dealt with him for years and years and years, and you know when he's not political he says 'Oh, I love Donald Trump, I love Donald Trump' but I will say— in fact, he came up to my office not so long ago to apologize because on his show, which is now off the air which is a fortunate thing, he called me a racist, and he came up, he literally came up to my office, and he apologized to me, which, by the way, I thought was very nice."

I've always been troubled by how I've personally gotten to know some of the right-wing conservatives—several of the Fox News hosts, for example—and have had more than one respectful, decent conversation with each. Off camera, we seem to be able to come to a respectful decision on how to operate with one another, with little personal animus in the mix. Yet, on television or in a magazine or newspaper article, these same personalities play to their right-wing audience using guys like me as their targets when they know better, including Donald Trump. It's easy to traffic in deception and distortion. It's far more difficult to speak the truth—it certainly doesn't make for biting headlines. It was one of the reasons it took me a long time to come to the public conclusion that Donald Trump is a racist. I know far too well how the right-wing media operates, and any opportunity to escalate division is a win for them.

It's ironic: of all the times in my life when I haven't held my tongue, this was the one moment when my efforts at moderation bit me. Perhaps I was waiting, as we all were, for Trump to rise to the occasion and become what we would consider *presidential*. I shouldn't have held my breath. When Trump raised the issue of birtherism, he crossed over from maintaining questionable opinions on sensitive matters to full-blown racism. It's an instance where the most outrageous headline also happens to be true: Trump Is a Racist. Whether Donald Trump sits up at night watching old reels of KKK films, I have no idea. It doesn't matter. He channels racism to cover and justify his other actions. He exploits the racism that festers deep in this country's history—an old wound not yet fully healed—and calls up its fearful anger to personal benefit. That Donald Trump is even comfortable with channeling racism makes him racist. The only apology owed is one to the American public: we deserve a president in office who speaks for all of us and doesn't peddle racism, homophobia, gender bias, or xenophobia.

As if that meeting in Trump Towers wasn't already strange, a few weeks later I would have another bizarre encounter with Trump at the taping of the *Saturday Night Live* Fortieth Anniversary Special where he and I were both guests. First I bumped into Sarah Palin on the red carpet, who was visibly uncomfortable making small talk with me live on national television. Moments like this remind me that, in many respects, New York is a small town where politics, entertainment, and the city's social life often overlap. As my girlfriend Aisha and I were walking to our seats, we ran into Trump. He grabbed my hand in his viselike grip and, pulling me close, smiled and said, "You do what you gotta do. I do what I gotta do." I realized then that he was committed. It didn't matter whether or not he himself personally believed in the birtherism movement: he was going to use it as political leverage to stoke fear and hate. He wasn't going after a headline. This reached much deeper. He saw the power that fear can inspire, and he was willing to bet his political and economic survival on it. If you're comfortable with promoting racism and being in the company of it, that either makes you a racist or a coward for not defending it. Trump is both. I was reminded of advice Coretta Scott King once gave me. She said, "Al, you cannot stand with people in the Black community who advocate violence and racism and, at the same time, advocate nonviolence. Association is assimilation. It's also an endorsement."

Four hundred years ago, this country was founded when the American colonies defied Britain. Four hundred years ago, African men, women, and children were forcibly taken from their land to help in that uniquely American endeavor. While Trump didn't birth racism, he has weaponized it for political effect and advantage. I don't know about yours, but my ancestors weren't looking for a better slave master. They were looking for freedom.

MORAL AUTHORITY

We may be witnessing a rise in nationalism as represented in its more proper form by President Trump and its far more ugly strain by white supremacists, but America isn't the only country grappling with its political identity. The rest of the world also seems to be in flux: the United Kingdom is facing its own turmoil with Brexit, and much of Europe is tackling their own homegrown versions of nationalism along with pressing immigration crises. I saw the killing of Iranian Major General Qasem Soleimani as related to this wave of global nationalism. When Trump announced that the United States would withdraw from the Joint Comprehensive Plan of Action (JCPOA), otherwise known as the "Iran nuclear deal," he didn't have another plan in place. The closest he had to a diplomatic plan was the assassination of the country's leading general.

Trump's premise for the killing—that the United States was in imminent danger from direct threats by Soleimani—broke down under scrutiny and left the American public with a sorry excuse for a killing that makes us no better than the Iranian nationalists themselves. We don't have the right or the moral authority to kill someone because he's a bad guy, even if he's a terrorist who has blood on his hands, unless that person is directly threatening our lives. This isn't to say that we can't use our military might to defeat terrorists and terrorism, but we certainly need to have a justified reason for pursuing that path. Otherwise, we've debased our political power and strength. Our war cries are the moral equivalent of a hard-core Iranian nationalist who wishes death on all Americans. As a country, we don't accept the right of foreign governments to kill our officials. Why would we permit the reverse? Why would we betray our moral standing in the world and permit our government to kill a foreign official? What makes us so special?

We *used* to be special: our economic and military strength was unrivaled. China has been chiseling away at our economic standing for years and, according to some measures, has already surpassed us. Our military is still unprecedented, but key players like Russia and China are gaining strength and in more tactical areas like cyber programs. North Korea has active and sophisticated nuclear weapons and ballistic-missile programs. More important than our economic and military power was this: America stood for something. Our global narrative was based on the idea that America was more than a country. It was an ideal, a dream, something to strive toward, cherish, and protect. We haven't always used our standing for good, but it was understood that America largely represented the global rule of law, and championed equality and decency among our allies. Our moral authority gave us our standing in the world. We, as Americans, prided ourselves on being decent, hardworking, and trustworthy; we'd never leave an ally out in the cold nor violate the rules of international law for the sake of political convenience. Under Trump's thumb, however, we've become a shell of our former selves: a self-interested, protectionist bully with little to no international credibility during a time when our interactions are more global than ever before.

Trump may have undercut our moral authority around the world, but the truth is we never lived up to it domestically anyway. We celebrated our authority and waved it around as proof of the superior decency of our self-proclaimed democracy. But we did not live up to it. How could we when the legacy of slavery gave us generations of men, women, and children who were threatened, beaten down, and abused? How could we when we denied women the right to vote and deny them equal rights still? How could we when we treated the immigrant family as the enemy rather than as someone to whom we "lift the lamp beside the golden door," as Emma Lazarus's famous sonnet reads on the pedestal of the Statue of Liberty? There were those among us, patriots like Lucy Stone, Frederick Douglass, and Martin Luther King Jr., who were trying to close the gap between our actions and our identity; that is, what we said and did and who we were. Unfortunately, we've found ourselves standing in that gap today, with our ideas and moral values positioned on one cliff and the reality of who we've become on another. The gap leaves room for bigots, homophobes, racists, and the like to fester. That gap birthed Donald J. Trump. It nurtured him, and he's profited off its immorality. He knew we haven't lived up to the promises of who we could be, and like any businessman looking for a bargain, he took advantage of that weakness, twisting and turning our collective failures into his personal gain.

Trump's base spoke up loud and clear when he was elected. Perhaps, in electing him, they decided that our moral standing in the world isn't as important as our national identity. The question is: Whose national identity? When we talk about national identity, are we talking about the people who live on Main Street, Wall Street, or Martin Luther King Jr. Boulevard? Are we talking about the 59.9 million Latinx who live in the United States? Are we talking about Deferred Action for Childhood Arrivals (DACA) recipients? We've always strived to live up to ourselves, to be a version of America that would inspire the world and make its citizens proud. If we're no longer engaged in that struggle, if we would rather give up on our ideals and embrace demagoguery and extreme nationalism, if we'd prefer to eat the best chocolate cake than hold fast to our morals, then ask yourself: Who reaps the benefits? Who gets rich off that trade?

As imperfect as we've been, even in the most difficult of times we've returned to ourselves. And so I say that the American experiment isn't dead, but it is struggling. I, for one, want to see America retain its moral authority and rededicate itself to the democratic experiment that made us unlike anywhere else in the world. Our real strength is derived from our core sense of moral identity and not our nationalistic impulses.

2

AN IMMORAL MAN IN A CHANGING WORLD:

Donald Trump, Latte Liberals, and Purity Politics

It's been widely reported by several respected news sources and outlets that Trump never wanted to be president. He himself didn't think he'd win and was rumored to have been preparing to concede when the numbers started turning in his favor. Trump's longtime buddy and former head of Fox News Roger Ailes used to say, "If you want a career in television, first run for president." I think Trump ran for president to expand his media empire and television presence, never expecting he'd soon be poring over approval numbers instead of Nielsen ratings.

The morning after the election, I woke in a state of shock. As I entered the lobby elevator of 30 Rockefeller Plaza on my way to the NBC Studios to prepare for my television show *PoliticsNation*, I gathered my resolve. I couldn't help but sense that something had shifted overnight. As a country, we were in new territory. Things were going to get real interesting, real quick. About a month later, while in a board meeting at NAN, my cell phone vibrated. Blocked number. Not thinking anything of it, I ignored the call. My phone vibrated again. This continued until I excused myself from the conference room to take the call outside.

A voice said, "Please hold for the president-elect."

Trump got on the phone, his voice full of bluster. "Al," he said, "can you believe it?" He went on, detailing the stats from his big win the night before. He told me that of all the people who would understand his win, I would. He always thought we were cut from the same cloth. Trump and I both came up in New York City during the 1980s and 1990s, a time when the tabloid was king. It's one of the reasons he and I understood each other. You've got to remember that most American cities had one or, if they were lucky, two prominent newspapers at that time, and maybe the same number of local television stations. New York City had six daily papers and a ton of television stations. In order for me to get media attention on civil rights issues—the 1986 murder of Michael Griffith in Howard Beach, Queens, for example—I had to do more than issue a press release to bring attention to the crime. It was only when I led a march of five hundred demonstrators to protest Griffith's murder that the media blinked and turned an eye toward the issue. I quickly learned that my personality could be a lightning bolt for good. My decision to publicize myself for the sake of the mission may have made me unpopular for life with some people, but it got my point across. To go full-court in our demand for justice, I also realized that I needed to engage the same dailies and journalists that Trump used to publicize the reopening of Wollman Rink in Central Park, for example. So, while I was organizing marches and protests, Trump was pretending to be his own media spokesperson, calling journalists to trumpet stories about his achievements, his sex life, or whatever new building featured his name in big gold letters.

Back in the day, I wasn't welcomed by New York's white power elite nor was Trump, though for totally different reasons. Much has been written about my medallions and tracksuits, my flashy sense of style. My contemporaries were entertainers and rappers, people like Russell Simmons and Public Enemy. Spike Lee and Betty Shabazz, Malcolm X's widow, were guests at the first rally I held in Harlem. In the context of Run DMC, I may have looked like an entertainer, but my audience was the congregation. What most people don't know is that the medallion I often sported in the 1980s—the one Rudy Giuliani told James Comey to bring to him as a trophy for protesting police brutality—was given to me as an award for my work in civil rights. So, let's be clear: I may have adopted the swagger of a showman—all the better to get eyeballs on the causes I was bringing into the light— but I also put in the work. In New York, Trump was seen as an entertainer of sorts, a guy who liked to throw his weight around and wanted the limelight all to himself. I can't say he's much different today.

I congratulated Trump on his win, and we hung up. It was a cordial enough call, but I didn't put much stock in it. I imagined he was going down a long list of names that morning, calling everyone he knew, singling out anyone who'd doubted him and gloating to everyone else. I wasn't sure what to make of our conversation except that it sounded like the Trump I knew: full of it. This was the same guy who'd promoted birtherism and who, along with his father, allegedly engaged in widespread housing discrimination against Blacks in the 1970s. This was the guy who openly denied justice to the Central Park Five, who bragged about sexual abuse...the list went on and on. *This* guy was the president-elect? My mind reeled, and a memory surfaced of a surreal encounter between Don King, Donald Trump, and me.

During the 1980s, Trump and King were friendly with each other, and I was friendly with Mike Tyson. Trump wanted Tyson to headline at one of his Atlantic City casinos, and so King arranged for us to meet. To my mind, Trump and King are the dons of self-promotion and the art of the transactional business deal. If King had been born white, he would have been Trump. They're both great at continuing to talk even if you're not talking back at 'em. It's amazing: they talk and talk and say absolutely nothing at the same time. So, when Trump, King, and I flew from New York City to Atlantic City on Trump's private helicopter, it was the longest ride of my life. I got an earful. Honestly, I can't even remember what was said 'cause both men were speaking over each other the entire time. It was the rare occasion when I shut up and marveled at the great swaths of land, factories, and train tracks that stretched between the two cities.

Trump ended up getting Tyson on contract, and in 1988, I attended the Tyson–Spinks fight at the Atlantic City Convention Hall in Atlantic City with Trump and his wife, Ivana. Promoted as the "once and for all" matchup, it was the richest fight in boxing history at the time. Trump worked with King to set it up and bid a record site fee of around $11 million to have it staged next to Trump Plaza. We took our seats, with Ivana sitting between Trump and me. Freddie Jackson, the Grammy-nominated R&B singer, was a friend of mine, and I'd gotten King to give him a shot singing the national anthem. As Freddie was singing, I leaned over to Ivana and told her that Freddie re-did the song "You Are My Lady." I continued, good-naturedly joking, "You know, it was your husband who got him to record that song and dedicate it to you." God forgive me. Trump didn't miss a beat. He passed off my lighthearted tease as truth, explaining that he'd forgotten to tell her about the song; he'd been so busy, it had slipped his mind, but wasn't she grateful he'd done that? Wasn't it a great gift? The greatest? It was a seemingly superfluous moment, but I've returned to it again and again in my mind since. It's funny: by telling her he forgot about the song, he set himself up for fault but then manipulated the lie into something grand, something beautiful. Like the best of the tabloid publishers, he can spin any narrative to suit his personal favor.

Donald Trump arrived at a unique moment in our country's history. In many respects, he's the first president of the social media era. Obama, of course, used social media for his benefit, too. But it took someone like Trump—a man already versed in the ways of the New York City tabloids—to exploit it. A natural showman, Trump fit in perfectly with the reality-television stars of the world. Like reality television itself, he's an expert at creating distraction and subterfuge, at playing to the highs and the lows of the crowd. He's one of the few public figures who can compete with a social media– and reality television–obsessed audience. Americans want charismatic leaders and heroes. Save for Bill Clinton and Obama, who, in his own way, was the epitome of cool, the Democrats have little in the way of charismatic leaders. Besides having a message, you need to know how to sell it, too. Anything less is difficult, maybe even impossible, to register with today's voters. Trump understands this and has made every effort throughout his life to be a personality with a capital P. I know this because I've been surrounded by big personalities most of my life. Whereas Trump got his lessons in manhood from men like his dad and Roy Cohn, I got mine from The Hardest Working Man in Show Business, Mr. James Brown, a man who knew how to make an entrance without needing a golden escalator.

Behind the glamor and the golden hair, here's the real deal on Trump: he's a Queens guy. It's as simple as that. He's either on the take or the make. Trump has never accepted his background. He needs the glitz to try to establish who he's not. He's never been comfortable in his skin. I have never—not once—had a meeting with Trump in which he seemed at ease, cool, or confident. This is a guy, born and raised in Jamaica Estates, Queens, whose family has never been considered part of the old, established guard of Manhattan. He may have been born with millions and erected buildings with his name plastered across them, but deep down he still feels the resentment of not being accepted into New York's elite circle of power brokers, most of whom viewed him as a joke—some still do. He was never *The New York Times*; he was always Page Six of the *New York Post*. Gossip and smear were part of his regular dealings as a New York City real-estate businessman, and he brought them into the White House, too. As former US Ambassador Gordon Sondland testified, Trump offered Ukraine a quid pro quo—the same way his builders say he withheld cash from them or any one of his competitors. Being president, however, isn't the equivalent of being a shady businessman; it's not the same thing to withhold aid to a foreign government while expecting them to dish up or fabricate information on a political rival.

Trump made a name for himself in New York City by clawing his way in and running the inside track on anyone who crossed him in business. He couldn't shake the fact, though, that he was outer-borough wealthy, and in New York, that made a difference. Compared to the high-stakes lifestyle of a Manhattan businessman, a real-estate developer from Queens was seen as ordinary and middle-class, maybe even a little provincial. On some level, this resentment set the stage for Trump's fevered us-against-them mentality. But the differences ran deeper, too.

With its stone-pillar entrance, tree-lined streets, and rows of imposing homes, the majority-white enclave of Jamaica Estates where Trump grew up was built for Queens's middle to upper-middle class. At the time of Trump's childhood, the neighborhood was heavily conservative and set apart from the rest of the borough, which was more economically varied and, further south, mostly Black. Though I was born and raised in Brooklyn, I lived part of my childhood in Hollis, Queens, near enough to Jamaica Estates but worlds apart. Neighborhoods in Queens were distinctly separate from one another and not at all equal. Boulevards like Jamaica, Hillside, and Union Turnpike were their own border walls and kept whites and minorities on opposite sides.

While Trump was dreaming of one day breaking down the doors of Manhattan's moneyed set, the Black community in Queens was being redlined into areas considered ineligible for mortgages backed by the Federal Housing Administration. Federally insured plans guaranteed smaller down payments and thirty-year payment plans, and other buyer-friendly terms that were denied most brown and Black and immigrant communities. By the late 1960s, racial segregation had become even more pronounced with an influx of Puerto Rican families arriving to the city and with the culmination of the mass migration of Blacks from the South. Most minorities were shut out of construction jobs and unions, and as the city moved from manufacturing jobs—half of which were lost—to service jobs, with a boom in the finance, insurance, and real-estate sectors, Black and brown communities lost out. When the teachers strike hit in 1968, a lot of white families left the city, setting up new all-white havens in Jersey, Westchester, and Long Island.

When Trump made it big in Manhattan—apartment on the Upper West Side, a Rolodex full of big shot names, gold-flecked furniture—he fulfilled that age-old, all-American story: he'd made it. There's a reason he and his third wife, Melania, danced to Frank Sinatra's "My Way" at his inaugural ball; it's the ultimate song of success and machismo for a certain type of clichéd New Yorker. He sold his presidential campaign to the American people by pitching himself as the ultimate insider-outsider, someone who understands what it's like to be close to the powerful and the elite but to not be one himself. He knows how to speak to the white family whose neighborhood is being encroached upon by minorities and immigrants. He knows how to speak to the disenfranchised white worker who dreams of a life of wealth and ease. He made good on the American dream and became rich and successful himself but never traded in his abrasive style—the elites couldn't break him. No one owned him. He was his own man. That's the headline anyway.

Trump isn't a career politician. He represents a certain cultural social dynamic that translates into politics. His lifestyle is recognizable. It's something seen on reality television, a real-life throwback to *Dynasty* or *Dallas*. People grow up watching someone like Trump make it in America—and make it big despite the bankruptcies, the extramarital affairs, and the discriminatory or criminal behavior of his companies—and they want to emulate him. Most politicians adhere to a certain Beltway mindset, following the herdlike mentality of so-called proper political thought, so that they forget that forty-nine of the states in America aren't in the Beltway. Trump's lack of political correctness is appealing to a certain group of people in this country—everyone from Roger Stone and Steve Bannon to the disenfranchised blue-collar worker—because they themselves feel shunned by the politically correct, a group I call the *latte liberals*, who hold tight to the academic principles of right and wrong, and act as if the conflicts we face in this country are nothing more than material for a stump speech. This kind of thinking—purity politics—is just as dangerous as Trump's obvious disdain for democratic norms.

THE RISE OF THE LATTE LIBERAL AND PURITY POLITICS

On April 12, 1963, Martin Luther King Jr. was arrested in Birmingham, Alabama, along with activists Ralph Abernathy, Fred Shuttlesworth, and other marchers. It was from his prison cell that Martin Luther King Jr. wrote the famous Letter from Birmingham City Jail, which was a response to a statement published in the local newspaper by eight white clergymen, who were firmly against Martin Luther King Jr.'s manner of protest. Martin Luther King Jr.'s measured yet fiery response wasn't directed toward the outright bigot; it was written for those moderate, Southern, liberal ministers who argued that now wasn't the time for him to rock the boat. Secure in their power and perhaps unconscious of it, these liberals couldn't understand the urgency of Martin Luther King Jr.'s push for change. When the white liberal tells the Black community and its leaders to wait and be patient, he not only appropriates the time line of the activist movement but also appropriates the protest itself. This is as true in 2020 as it was in 1963. There's never an appropriate time to protest. To suggest otherwise goes against the very nature of what a protest is. If there's no problem, there's no reason to protest. When the white ally elects himself to be the gatekeeper, someone who effectively signals what is or isn't acceptable to the status quo, he becomes part of the problem itself. Today's latte liberal, whether conscious or not, does everything to protect the status quo.

Much of what today's politicians talk about doesn't hit the ground with where people are. From Florida to Iowa to California, Americans are worried about how to put food on the table, pay their bills, and protect their children. After the devastating effects of COVID-19, these are front-burner issues, with small businesspeople, mom-and-pop storeowners, and gig economy workers struggling to get back to a place of normalcy. Yet, political talk is dominated both by spin and high-brow ideas that have no real bearing on the life of the average American family, Black or white. This is an example of latte liberalism—the talk sounds good, but it's not action-based, and it certainly doesn't engender change for the communities that need it the most. It's a form of liberalism that smacks of privilege and cocoons itself by staying out of touch with the messiness that often accompanies real hardship, like the struggle of trying to make ends meet, dealing with a family member in prison or addicted to opioids, or struggling to cover the costs of burying a loved one.

In my experience, most of the latte liberals I encounter are white, and their sense of privilege makes it nearly impossible to speak with them about institutionalized racism. They can address blatant racism with ease—and can spout data about advances made under the civil rights movement or the Obama administration. They may even be sensitive to the racialized components of being born Black in America and know the lyrics to a Jay-Z song, but they're rarely willing to openhandedly fess up to the racism that has made their lives inordinately better than the lives of their Black and brown friends. They're certainly reluctant to share the advantages their whiteness confers. I'm talking about the decades-long history of advantages—zoning laws, bank loans, and education initiatives—that have effectively protected them from some of life's messier realities. A latte liberal may mean well, but his lack of empathy or understanding of the basic inequalities that go hand in hand with bigotry, racism, and economic disparity make him suspect to anyone struggling to get a foothold in the American dream. I'd go so far as to say that if latte liberals had a better sense of these issues and their Black and brown and immigrant brothers, there'd be no need for someone like me. There probably wouldn't have been a need for a Donald Trump either: if latte liberals, the majority of whom are elitist and interested only in maintaining the status quo, hadn't been so quick to dismiss the very real fears and anxieties of the so-called forgotten men and women of rural Americana, blue-collar workers and otherwise, Trump would have never risen to become president.

During his election campaign and throughout his presidency, Trump addressed the fears of his white base—albeit in the most profane, cynical, and manipulative manner possible. He used their fear for his own political benefit, stoking it and giving it a place, a voice on the nation's political stage. If this group felt neglected before the 2016 Trump election, he made sure they felt heard and validated afterwards. Think about it: in 2016, the economy was humming along—at least on Wall Street—yet the average American sensed that, somehow, the numbers didn't add up, not in rural Appalachia or in coal-mining country, not in Cleveland, Ohio, or in Baltimore, Maryland, where the wages were stagnant, manufacturing jobs were gone or dwindling, and most people worked two or three jobs. Forget about retirement savings. Trump presented himself as a fighter for the underdogs, someone who'd been kicked down by multiple bankruptcies but dreamed big and got back on top.

This lack of empathy for the white lower class isn't exclusive to the liberal set—far from it. Conservatives and Republicans are just as guilty. In January 2019, Fox News host Tucker Carlson addressed the problems specific to rural white America, the base of the Republican voters, saying, "Stunning out-of-wedlock birthrates. High male unemployment. A terrifying drug epidemic. How did this happen? You'd think our ruling class would be interested in knowing the answer. But mostly they're not. They don't have to be interested. It's easier to import foreign labor to take the place of native-born Americans who are slipping behind." Republicans now represent white rural voters or those who live in towns and cities where the once-booming, male-dominated manufacturing jobs have largely evaporated and, with them, the unions, the weekend company baseball leagues, the salary and the respect, you name it. While white elitism can be found in both parties, it doubles as purity politics in the Democratic Party and can be just as toxic as some of the outright racism of the Republican Party.

Purity Politics

It's both a political and moral mistake to position oneself as being pure as Caesar's wife, because no one is. At our core, we're fundamentally flawed. I don't trust anyone who hasn't been through some stuff or isn't empathetic to someone's struggle. If we recognize that none of us can pass a purity test, then why does the Democratic Party and the liberal-elite media keep dishing them out? These arbitrary litmus tests— you have to think or act a certain way, have the so-called right degree or résumé, have donated to the right groups or organizations, et cetera—enforces the very us-versus-them mentality that undermine the Party's larger goals. If you take such a hard line for your morality, how is there ever going to be room for political negotiation on any topic that has to appeal to a wide range of people? In a politically divisive time, Trump flouts the very notion of a purity test. He knows he's no standard-bearer of good behavior. Instead, he indulges in crassness, passing off derogatory statements as something everyone's thinking but only he has the courage to say aloud. He traffics in scandal, all the more to make his constituents feel that any scandal or fault of their own is excusable. He revels being with the sinners not because he recognizes our shared human capacity for being flawed individuals but because he can co-opt bad behavior as a way to further and excuse his own.

Change requires intersectionalism and inclusivity, working toward common ground. You have to make up your mind: Are you trying to bring change or are you trying to be pure? To raise this idea a notch further: If your purity tests get in the way of achieving greater moral change, isn't your so-called purity amoral? I'm reminded of the James 2:26 passage: "For as the body without the spirit is dead, so faith without works is dead also." People who go to mosques or temples or churches every day may be pious and prayerful, but what work do they do? What service? Some people approach their politics in a similar fashion, thinking grand ideas but not putting in real, on-the-ground work to help level the playing field for everyone. If we are to reform and redirect the energy of this country, politicians must meet people where they are, not where we want them to be. Otherwise, we're simply forcing people to rise up to some meaningless, arbitrary standard that doesn't hold real water anyway.

Whether you live in Roanoke, Virginia, or Brooklyn, New York, you have more in common with your fellow American than you think. The politicians we want working in our state capitols and in our local communities are those men and women who understand the real needs of the average American. Politicians who are more interested in maintaining the status quo or in having academic debates with one another are doing a disservice to the American people. They're useless and irrelevant. The politics of demographics divides us and only serves the status quo, keeping the people in power exactly where they want to be: in control of those who are not. If we're locked in a battle of demographic politics, we're no different than the people we oppose, and no one accomplishes anything.

Colin Kaepernick:
Taking a Knee to Take a Stand

As a young preacher, one of the first books my mentor Reverend William Jones recommended I read was Reinhold Niebuhr's *Moral Man and Immoral Society*, in which the author argued that if you live in an immoral society, you become a part of a system that executes and enforces immorality. We're living in an era in which we emphasize the importance of personal morality but institutionalize inequity. Occasionally, however, a man takes a stand.

I don't know former San Francisco 49ers quarterback Colin Kaepernick personally, but when he took a knee during the national anthem to protest alleged police brutality and racial inequality, he stood for civil rights. To do what he did at the height of public scrutiny took courage and conviction. It was the clear result of a man exercising his moral authority in a world that desperately wanted him to look away and not confront its immorality. He didn't. He couldn't. The public outrage that followed was predictable, painful, and came at great personal and professional cost. It reminded me of the statement from the white Southern ministers to Martin Luther King Jr. in Birmingham when they told him to wait and be patient. Since when is a protest ever convenient or appropriate? Appropriate for whom? When is it the right time for moral outrage to raise its head and speak the truth? Trump, as he is so skilled at doing, co-opted the Kaepernick movement as a wedge issue. But let's not forget: if there was no need for a protest to occur—if there was no such thing as police brutality against Blacks—then Kaepernick wouldn't have had the idea to take a knee in the first place. But it does, and he did.

By taking a knee, Kaepernick elevated the issue of racial inequality to the level of the National Football League. He moved it front and center and gave it a stage on prime time. It was a beautiful display of silent protest and reminded me of everything I learned from the leaders of the civil rights movement, and from Reverend Jones in particular: Kaepernick never gave in to violence to make his point nor did he say anything bigoted or spiteful. Instead, he maintained his dignity and kept his integrity. His protest was the embodiment of the values and the spirit of resistance that has informed decades of civil dissent in this country. In the wake of George Floyd's death, I've been heartened that so many protesters around the world have followed Kaepernick's model. George may have died with a police officer's knee to his neck, but in kneeling in peace, the protesters are rising up for justice in his name.

As a living example of how to do the right thing, Kaepernick put the calling—the cause—before his career. So many of us, politicians included, do the opposite, even when we know better. He may not ever play again—I hope he does—but he'll be more well-known than any other player in his generation because of what he stood for. He reminds me of Muhammad Ali in some respects.

Ali was one of the most hated figures in sports when he refused to sign up for military service in 1967. For three years, he could not make a living. And yet, he's remembered today as a man, a champion, who didn't yield his integrity to the crowd. He did what was right and, at the end of his career, reaped the benefits and accolades of the same people who only a few years prior had dismissed his values. Kaepernick, like Ali, is proof that it's possible, even necessary, to be the inverse of Trump; that is, a moral man in an ever-changing, sometimes painfully immoral world.

DIVISION WITHIN: MODERATES VERSUS PROGRESSIVES

If the Republican Party today largely represents the white voter, the Democratic Party is dependent on the Black vote. We saw this bear out with the most recent Democratic Party presidential primaries as the Black vote swung heavily in Joe Biden's favor. Even though I expected Biden to do well, he did better than I thought he would. I think Biden's win against Bernie Sanders on Super Tuesday shocked everyone clustered inside the progressive silo, and that's because a lot of Democrats in general don't understand the Black vote. Biden won because of the Black vote. As a group, the progressives often overlook our strength because so many of them speak at us rather than to us. There are exceptions, of course. In 2018, NAN invited the Democratic nominees to our annual conference. I was absolutely stunned by Elizabeth Warren's high-energy performance. She was like a Baptist preacher, calling people to their feet. She commanded the stage and was as passionate as she was authentic. After many of the other nominees left—moving on to the next photo op—Liz went into the crowd to take selfies and to engage in one-on-one conversations for the next hour and a half. She did the same thing in 2019 at the next NAN conference.

Most high-level politicians appoint their chummy colleagues and old friends to positions of Black leadership without realizing that they should be electing leaders from the Black community, people who can speak to the issues that affect them most. I'm not criticizing to belittle them. I'm criticizing to raise the point: the progressive agenda can be fully realized if its leaders learn to speak to us, the Black community. The average Black voter is more centrist on issues not having to do with race. They aren't driven to the polls by political theory, socialist ideas, or talk of revolution. The Black voter is concerned with making sure their family's basic needs are cared for: health insurance, education, job stability, and retirement. This isn't to say, however, that they're against the progressive agenda; there's a way to talk about the goals of the progressive party that make them appealing to everyone, not just to the latte liberals. The progressives also underestimated the legacy of Barack Obama, whom Black voters have a deep appreciation for and a real sense of pride in. In many ways, Obama was more progressive than Biden ever was, and yet Biden gets to carry the mantle of his legacy.

The Black vote turned the Democratic nomination process into a race. Besides Warren taking Bloomberg to task for buying his way into the race and his supposed history of treating women poorly, the former mayor's campaign was also stumped by his past policy of stop-and-frisk, a Black-voters' issue, and his handling of the Central Park Five. So, years later, the very issues that I was castigated, lampooned, and cartooned for are the same ones that bring down a billionaire candidate. In 2012, NAN brought together other civil rights and labor union groups, like GLAAD, New York–based Service Employees International Union (SEIU), and the National Association for the Advancement of Colored People (NAACP), and thousands of us marched thirty blocks from Harlem to Bloomberg's home off Fifth Avenue to protest the stop-and-frisk program. In 2011 alone, the police stopped 685,000 men, most of whom were either Black or Latino; only 10 percent were found guilty of any crime. Who would have thought, when I planned that silent march eight years ago, that stop-and-frisk would become a major issue in a presidential race? That's when you know activism works. That's when you know you've changed the conversation. Pete Buttigieg also struggled to connect with the Black voter, in part because of his poor relationship with the community in his hometown of South Bend, Indiana, and, in part, because of some of the homophobia in our community toward an openly gay candidate, something I address in Chapter Three.

We've seen, time and time again, that the Black vote matters. Why, then, does the Democratic Party and its liberal base keep failing the Black community? Why does the Democratic politician continue to stand by policies that promote discriminatory and institutional inequity? The Democrats' failing of the Black community, however, doesn't vindicate the Republicans—far from it. The Republican Party wrote off the Black community years ago. Just because you're in an abusive relationship doesn't mean you leave only to submit yourself to a pimp. You leave to find something better, more healthy. One of the reasons I ran for president in 2004 was because I thought the Democratic Party needed to be challenged, and

I'm not solely talking about the moderates. In creating the atmosphere that they're somehow the supposed purists of the party, the progressives have wrongly assumed that this gives them the permission and the authority to speak on behalf of the community. If you want to know what the Black community wants and needs, here's an idea: help lift the voices of the leaders already positioned inside that community.

During the earliest days of voter-zoning laws in New York City, many of the Black neighborhoods were divided up to favor white representatives, many of whom often didn't live in the same neighborhoods they supposedly represented. It took years of championing Black leaders from the ground up and challenging the district-zoning laws for a Black community to be represented by one of their own. It is absolutely critical to the success of the Black community to have leaders who speak for them. It's one of the reasons no one can shut me up.

I think Tom Perez, chair of the Democratic National Committee, has done a great job in trying to address the issue of diversity within the Party, but he's dealing with the mechanisms of an institution that takes time to turn around. Perez has a long career history in fighting for diversity. Unfortunately, as the face of the DNC, he gets much of the blame rather than the state and national politicians who loathe change. Still, when I look at the two white men who were the last of the Democratic nominees, Biden and Sanders, both of whom are over the age of seventy, I wonder what the average Black or Latino or Asian American family thinks of their lack of representation on the national stage. I, of course, championed Pete Buttigieg's presence for the LGBTQ community and Elizabeth Warren and Amy Klobuchar for representing the country's dominant majority population: women. But what does it say that the minority candidates—Andrew Yang, Kamala Harris, and Corey Booker—were missing in the final count? Can a white politician relate to the everyday issues of the Black, brown, and immigrant family? And if they cannot, are they willing to work twice as hard to confront those harsh realities on behalf of the people who so desperately need a voice? Are they willing to appoint members to their cabinet to help them with this task?

When I attended the January 2020 Democratic debate in Iowa, there was plenty of latte liberalism on display with everything—from international issues to impeachment—up for grabs. There was no conversation about criminal-justice reform, policing issues, or the rise in hate crimes—issues that run to the very heart of the Democratic base of Black and brown families. This is why Trump wins: he speaks directly to his base. Democrats talk past their base. We're in real danger if the Democratic leadership continues to talk at people rather than to them. In order to speak to someone, you must also listen to them—all the better to understand the root of their fear and anxiety, their hope. Obama knew this and harnessed his campaign accordingly. The Democratic Party has certainly expanded its base since Obama's first election. But can we hold that expansion during the era of Trump and broaden it even more? Can the progressive wing of the Democratic Party work with and talk to the moderate wing and vice versa? Can we bring the people together?

Much of the progressive agenda and issues that are dear to a vast majority of Americans are now front and center. People talk openly about LGBTQ rights and sexism today. There's an awareness of white privilege and how it confers certain advantages. We're beginning to discuss the idea of reparations. These are issues that even a few years ago weren't mainstream talk, certainly not on the presidential stage. In this sense, the party has been moving in a more progressive direction whether or not we've actively realized it. The Democratic Party is catching up to itself. Senators Bernie Sanders and Elizabeth Warren took the energy of Occupy Wall Street to a national level. The danger now is that we eat our own children. A movement is about addition, not subtraction; we can't afford infighting within our own Party.

I'm reminded of the Judgment of Solomon, the famous Biblical story in which King Solomon of Israel ruled in the case of two women both claiming to be the mother of a child. In trying to appeal to the women's idea of fairness, he declared his judgment: the baby would be cut in two, with each woman to receive half. One mother didn't contest the ruling, saying that if she couldn't have the child, then neither of them could. The other mother, however, begged Solomon to spare the child. She preferred to give the child to the other woman than have him killed. The king declared the second woman as the true mother, as a mother would even give up her baby if it meant saving his life. The Democratic Party must come to terms with itself; we can't afford to sacrifice the gains nor dismiss the grievances of the progressives while adopting Biden as the presumptive moderate nominee. In 2016, we traded in the momentum of Obama's transformational leadership—his eight years in power—for Trump's transactional style. Let's not do it again.

Reconciliation

As we do every year, on January 20, 2020, the National Action Network hosted a celebration to honor Martin Luther King Jr. Former President Bill Clinton was our featured guest. On that Monday morning, I woke early and did the *Morning Joe* show. The panel and I were talking about Martin Luther

King Jr.'s legacy, and I said, "Dr. King, in his last four or five years, had become more unpopular than popular, according to polls of Black Americans, yet he remained steadfast, loyal, and faithful to his core beliefs of nonviolent and direct-action tactics. I think that that is something we miss today as people who take a moral stand on what is popular not on what they believe, and he believed in trying to reconcile society. He believed that there should be social movements but that they should end in reconciliation."

While making my way uptown from the studio, I thought about Martin Luther King Jr.'s notion of reconciliation. It's ironic: in the 1980s, I was part of the progressive wing of the Democratic Party that challenged the centrists' move of Bill Clinton and Al Gore and their creation of the Democratic Leadership Council. This council was formed, in part, to combat the fear that the Party had gone too left. I argued that the Party couldn't afford to become centrist. We didn't lose with Mondale or Dukakis because we were too left; we lost because of the Reagan–Bush, silent-majority Christian right, which we needed to counter and not succumb to. This was part of the rationale as to why I ran in 2004: I felt that the Democrats were behaving as elephants wearing donkey sheets. Fast-forward some twenty years later, and I'm about to share the NAN stage with Clinton.

It says something about how polarized we've become in this country when Bill Clinton and I can share a political affinity because while we're of different minds, we can at least still agree on the kind of America worth fighting for. Progressives and centrists alike can reconcile themselves to a common vision of America, a place where everyone is invited to the table, and justice makes waste of hatred and bigotry. In this sense, Donald Trump has brought us together. Because he and his administration and the Republican Party have failed to denounce hatred, basic inequalities, and white nationalism in any meaningful way, because of their disregard of truth and facts, the Democrats now face a reckoning of our own. To my mind, the choice is pretty clear: Do you go the way of the demagoguery or of democracy? The Democratic Party was unable to reconcile itself in 2016, and it helped Trump. We don't have to demonize the progressive or centrist sides of the Democratic Party. To do so only weakens our standing and further erodes core beliefs common to both sides.

While I spent the day memorializing Martin Luther King Jr.'s vision and life, progun groups were simultaneously marching in Virginia. Fringe militia groups were organizing online and off-line. Do we want to fight the progressive agenda versus the centrist one? Or do we want to mobilize our efforts to help address the bigger picture? The president of the United States didn't address the nation in any substantive way for Martin Luther King Jr. Day, preferring instead to have a quick photo-op at the Martin Luther King Jr. Memorial on the National Mall. I was reminded of something King once said: "Every man must decide whether he will walk in the light of creative altruism or in the darkness of destructive selfishness." I am hopeful that we will find light in today's dark times.

Many Americans are looking to Joe Biden to lead us out of the darkness. I first dealt with Joe in the 1990s when, as senator, he was one of the authors of the 1994 Omnibus Crime Bill. I felt the legislation went too far and was too punitive—there was mandatory sentencing for crack but not the same sentencing against individuals selling cocaine. He and I tussled over the bill and Clinton's welfare reform acts. Even when we were on opposite sides of an issue, however, Joe was always respectful. He's a straight shooter and in DC that's incredibly rare. While we certainly need a leader who can respectfully unite the separate factions of the America politic into a cohesive coalition, that leader will only be as strong as we are ourselves.

Barack Obama:
Transformational Leadership

January 20 was not only the day before Martin Luther King Jr. Day but in 2013, it also marked the start of Inaugural Weekend, with Obama's public swearing-in ceremony planned the following day. As if this weren't enough, it also marked the 175th anniversary of the founding of one of the oldest Black churches in Washington, DC, the Metropolitan A.M.E. Church. Such a confluence of events seemed divine directed. Reverend Roland E. Braxton preached a memorable sermon and spoke about the exodus of the Israelites from Egypt and the need to move forward when forward is the only option. Later, Martin Luther King III and I, along with others, lay a wreath at the Martin Luther King Jr. Memorial. As we did, we hoped that Obama's second term would continue to represent Martin Luther King Jr.'s legacy, and not just symbolically but also in policy. The following morning, my girlfriend and I made our way to St. John's Episcopal Church for mass. It's not every day that you're seated next to Elie Wiesel and Martin Luther King III. However, this was no ordinary day at church. After mass, we made our way to the US Capitol for the inauguration.

Unlike Obama's first inauguration, this time I was seated on the official inaugural platform, surrounded by members of the US Senate and House of Representatives and other luminaries, political and otherwise. The Supreme Court justices and the Biden family sat a row in front of me. Beyoncé and Martin Luther King III were nearby. Senator Chuck Schumer caught my attention, saying, "You have better seats than me!" Senator John McCain overheard our banter and approached. Now, McCain and I have had our share of disagreements over the years, but on that day, we talked about his daughter, Meghan. Before she became one of the co-hosts of *The View*, I often invited her to appear on my show, where she and I would debate the topics of the day. Senator McCain thanked me for treating her with respect. I explained that whatever difference of opinion I may have with someone, it's not personal. I can disagree with someone and still respect them. I went on to say that I'd want him to show my daughters the same level of respect, which I knew he would. From that day forward, McCain and I were a bit more friendly with one another. While the loftiness of that day may have inspired our mutual admiration, I have to think we also brought it out in each other. Congresswoman Shirley Chisholm used to say, "You'll find people going your way may not go to the same church as you. You may not dress the same. You may not eat the same. But it's wise to put those differences aside to recognize a fellow traveler." As I looked around the inaugural platform, I couldn't help but notice my fellow travelers—Republicans and Democrats alike. Obama's words echoed inside my mind: "What makes us exceptional— what makes us American—is our allegiance to an idea articulated in a declaration made more than two centuries ago: 'We hold these truths to be self-evident, that all men are created equal; that they are endowed by their Creator with certain unalienable rights; that among these are life, liberty, and the pursuit of happiness.' Today we continue a never-ending journey to bridge the meaning of those words with the realities of our time."

I couldn't shake the feeling of how improbable it was that I, Reverend Al Sharpton, would be in attendance on that historical day. If my mother didn't already have dementia and I told her about my morning, she wouldn't have believed me. Later, I thanked the president and told him it was an honor to have been invited into that circle. In his cool and collected way, he simply responded, "Of course," like it was no big thing. His attitude and response confirmed what I already knew about Barack: if you were with him, committed to your work, and authentic, he was with you, too. He brought people up instead of trying to keep them down, and that's the quality of a truly transformational leader. I believe his leadership style grew out of his unique personal background and childhood.

Barack Obama, as the child of an interracial marriage, was positioned from birth to see both sides of a given situation. Raised as a Black man by white grandparents and a white mother, Obama spent most of his childhood in Honolulu, Hawaii, but also spent time in Indonesia before settling in Chicago, Illinois, where he worked as a community organizer and lawyer while lecturing on constitutional law at the University of Chicago Law School. As a young man, Obama had to figure out his own identity in the midst of different identities and family components. His Black father was largely absent from his life and, so, while he knew of his Blackness, he wasn't fully immersed in its culture. This unique upbringing gave him, at a young age, the freedom and the capacity to create who he wanted to be in his own mind because that identity wasn't reflected in his immediate environment. I think it also gave him the ability later in life to create a new political paradigm.

Obama had firsthand experience in cribbing together his own identity, one based on several seemingly discordant personalities but that, in fact, made up a whole greater than the sum of its parts. The fact that he had the wherewithal and the intellectual curiosity to define himself in a way that balanced the various influences of his life also gave him the latitude to create a new political model for America. He didn't come out of a fixed world where his Blackness defined him. To a degree, he was forced to define what Blackness meant to him; his was an expansive mindset, and it opened the playing field. Instead of thinking it was outrageous for a Black man to run against Hillary Clinton for the Democratic nomination, he thought *Why not?* It's what made Barack Obama a dreamer. There was nothing about him that fit in the normal experience of being a Black man in America; his upbringing was unconventional, and he was, too. With the freedom of not having to conform to other people's expectations, he could make up his own ideas of success, and he did. Rather than changing himself to fit America, he changed America. There's a difference between a dreamer like Obama, who created his own world, and a schemer like Trump, who tries to figure out how to be the biggest guy, the most successful guy, the winner, in a world that's already been rigged for him.

Obama's success is that he tapped into our higher selves, the idea of who we want to be. People wanted hope. People wanted to believe the United States was the kind of place where a Black man, despite our history of slavery and our past and current struggles with racism and bigotry, could be elected president. That's the stuff of dreams. The undercurrent of racism that threatens to destroy his signature policies and legislative efforts is corruption at its most base. Obama isn't hope itself, but he is its personification just as Trump personifies the dangers of transactional leadership.

INTERSECTIONALISM

As president, Barack Obama was able to intersect some of what was going on in the Democratic Leadership Council with the more progressive left. He gave a certain comfort level to both, while elevating the game itself. In this sense, he was the definition of a transformational leader. People understood—then and now—that Obama wasn't your ordinary politician. He was a different breed, someone who was truly invested in transforming our democracy into a fully functional system, one that not only addressed big-picture issues of human rights, climate change, and income inequality but also brought us closer to reconciling the pain and struggles of our past. Some of the secret to Obama's success was that he resisted the temptation to be a purist; he spoke plainly when he needed to and wasn't dogmatic in his tactics. In this way, he was able to bring together the best attributes of the Democratic Party, and he tempered his personality accordingly. Most importantly, he was fluent in intersectionalism and coalition politics.

Obamacare—or the Affordable Care Act—is a great example of how intersectionalism can work. Obama worked with a number of different agencies, organizations, and individuals all across the board to form alliances based on the shared goal of providing insurance to Americans. It remains the health care system's most significant regulatory overhaul and expansion of coverage since Medicare and Medicaid passing in 1965. I was privileged to watch Obama negotiate these alliances up close because I had developed a working relationship with his phenomenal senior advisor Valerie Jarrett. Valerie understood government and the power of community, and demonstrated more integrity to me than anyone I've encountered in government since.

Obama didn't learn about intersectionalism or how to create government alliances at Harvard. He learned it from being a community organizer in Chicago. He learned it from being on the ground, listening to real people about their real concerns. It's good to talk to the pollsters, but it's just as beneficial to speak with the doormen and the drivers, the cleaning women and the garbage collectors, because it's important to get a sense of what life is like for working people on the street. Obama knew how to traverse both worlds and knit them together.

We've got to deal with the intersectionalism of all our causes. In many respects, I started NAN as a kind of continuation of Jesse Jackson's Rainbow Coalition. I believe in the idea of stitching different patches of the American quilt together. It's the only way we're going to save ourselves. It doesn't work if you're on your own because there's not enough in your one little patch, but if everyone comes together based on their own self-interests and a shared sense of common values and principles, we become the majority. That was the bold claim of the American experiment. Nowhere else in the history of the world has any other country committed itself to such high principles—all men are created equal and, at the same time, bring me your huddled masses—so that we would build a society of different people, nationalities, and races, which is why if we fail, the rest of the world will say it can't be done. We have to do this not only for the salvation of our own national soul, but to say to the world, *yes, it can be done.* Otherwise, you're telling the rest of the world to embrace their monarchs and dictators, to give in to the destructive nature of tribalism. I'm not willing to accept that; I refuse to allow the lowest base of our humanity to dictate my future and the future of generations to come. I believe that the human family has the capacity to live in such a way that appeals to our higher sense of purpose and innate goodness.

As a country, I believe we were moving in a certain direction under the Obama administration. We were learning how to accept people with equal protection under the law and opportunity—the tenets of which our country itself proclaimed were our birthright even if we'd yet to live up to those ideals. I believe we were moving closer toward fulfilling the promise of the American experiment. Trump rose on the backbone of white America, mobilizing the fears of a population afraid of the loss of power that comes with righting inequity. At the same time, the Democratic Party isolated itself from this group, and even went so far as to call this demographic *deplorables.* The average white American, racist or not, felt excluded and judged by this subtle form of progressive elitism. Here's the truth: people do not have to qualify to some self-imposed standard in order to rise up. They do not have to belong to a certain income bracket or reach a certain level of education. They don't have to conform to a certain social etiquette. They don't even have to belong to the same church or come from the same sexual orientation. *Rise up* means everyone comes to the table. *Rise up* means everyone gets out of their respective comfort zones and lifts each other.

FIGHTING DIRTY

In 2019, the National Action Network hosted fifteen of the Democratic presidential nominees at our annual convention where Congressman Tim Ryan told a moving story about Muhammad Ali that I'd never heard before.

Seeing Ali on the street, a man called out, "Hey, champ, I saw you get knocked out at the Garden. You were flat on your back." He laughed and jeered to his friends.

Ali said, "Wasn't me."

The man continued, "What are you talking about? Of course it was you. I saw it. I had ringside seats."

Ali said, "No, you either saw me standing or getting up. I've never stayed down."

This is the kind of attitude we need right now in the struggle to reclaim our country's moral compass. It may feel daunting—the courts are loaded with Trump's conservative picks; monumental legislation and policies are being rolled back daily; Trump gives rambling, free-form press conferences chock-full of misinformation on the dangers of a global pandemic—but we can't surrender the fight. We can't stay down. The opposition would love it if we gave up. In fact, their strategy demands it of you, because if you give up, nothing changes. If you allow your spirit to be broken, the fight's over. No matter what they keep hitting you with, you keep going because you have no other choice. None.

People who fight dirty don't last. The dirty fighters are in it for the crowd, the self-adulation, the quick win. They don't know how to play the long game. Trump is the dirtiest fighter there is. Give him an opening and he'll hit below the belt. There's no point in enumerating the low blows he's dealt; the list would be too long. But after a while, the crowd starts to catch on. The audience knows when the game is rigged, when it's unfair. Trump has gaslighted us into believing that it's rigged against him, but I believe that the American public will see through this ruse. The con-man routine has been Trump's bread and butter for the past fifty-odd years. He sees everyone as a con man because he himself is always in on the con. It's inconceivable to him that people have beliefs or core principles beyond the hustle because he lacks them himself. He assumes that everyone is on the take and can be bought, because he's always been up for sale. He thinks everyone is amoral and has ulterior motives, because he has only ever been amoral himself. But there's another way.

The minister in me always hopes for a miracle, and while I wasn't surprised by Trump's impeachment acquittal, I was disappointed. From the ashes of the impeachment, however, two individuals rose up with admirable courage and voted to convict Trump: Alabama Senator Doug Jones and Utah Senator Mitt Romney. My mother was born and raised in Alabama. My stepsister, stepbrother, and brother-nephew live in Alabama today. It's a state I know well. Doug Jones stood up on principle where political expedience would have told him to do otherwise. I think his voters would have understood if he had sided with the Republicans, and yet he didn't. I have tremendous respect for what he did. Likewise for Mitt Romney. I gave him hell when he ran in 2012. He and I obviously have different politics, but I still respect the fact that he stood up to the courage of his convictions.

Two years after Martin Luther King Jr.'s death, my high school dedicated a memorial plaque to the civil rights leader. The quote that appeared on the plaque read: "The ultimate measure of a man is not where he stands in moments of comfort and convenience, but where he stands at times of challenge and controversy." I believe Jones and Romney showed the strength of their character in taking the stand they did.

My hope is that as more Americans—Republican, Democrat, progressive, and moderate—rise up, the immoral society corroding our political system will give way to a unified coalition stronger than a sea of red MAGA hats.

3

STANDING FIRM:

Faith, Community, and Civil Rights

Ten days before leaving the office of the White House, President Barack Obama called a meeting with civil rights organizations and leaders who had worked with him during his eight years in power—the National Urban League, the NAACP, Representative John Lewis, myself, and others, including a few young activists. We met in the Roosevelt Room. I sat beside Lewis and Valerie Jarrett and took in what felt like our Last Supper. While I'd visited the White House some seventy times over the course of Obama's two terms, this meeting, situated as it was on the eve of his farewell, was especially moving and bittersweet. As I mentally catalogued some of the administration's strongest accomplishments—the Affordable Care Act, the President's Task Force on 21st Century Policing, and efforts to fight voting suppression—I couldn't help but think of my mother, Ada Essie Sharpton, and wondered if I had done enough to help.

Much of what we'd accomplished was now at stake—and this fear, this dawning realization, stretched back further in history than the past eight years. I looked at Representative John Lewis, who was beaten by Alabama state troopers and almost died on the Edmund Pettus Bridge in Selma, Alabama, marching for voting rights in 1965. Some of these rights and wins were already subject to attack even while Obama was in office. In 2013, for example, the Supreme Court dismantled a key pillar of the 1965 Voting Rights Act. The court's conservative majority ruled that the government was using an outdated process to determine which states were required to have their voting rules approved by the government, making it harder for Blacks and other minorities to vote. At the time, Attorney General Eric Holder said the decision was "a serious setback for voting rights," especially in places where voting discrimination has been historically prevalent. Under the pretext of voter fraud, Republicans have long aimed to roll back laws put in place to protect minorities and students—two demographics who tend to vote Democrat. Once Trump was in office, armed with a majority-led Senate, and a soon-to-be conservative Supreme Court, I had little doubt that voter suppression, purges, and gerrymandering would accelerate, and they have.

Studies have shown that when voter turnout increases, Republican victories decrease. Voter suppression has only gained strength under the Trump administration. Republicans from states like Wisconsin and Georgia and beyond have purged hundreds of thousands of voters from their rolls, disproportionately targeting voters of color. In June 2020, Kansas's Republican Attorney General Derek Schmidt sought to appeal a 10th US Circuit Court of Appeals decision that said the state couldn't enforce a proof-of-citizenship law for first-time voters. If the US Supreme Court takes the case, the decision would broadcast beyond Kansas because Alabama, Arizona, and Georgia also have proof-of-citizenship laws. Today, our voting system is also under threat from cyberattack, and yet little has been done to combat the proven vulnerabilities of our voting machines and registration infrastructure. And, as if this wasn't enough, the 2020 census has redistricting implications for the next decade.

It's easy to have hindsight bias, but it was undeniable that every person in that room felt the weight of history on their shoulders. Voting rights weren't the only protections up for grabs. We knew that Trump would go after so much more, and he has: his Economic Growth, Regulatory Relief and Consumer Protection Act undermines our nation's key civil rights laws and weakens consumer protections enacted after the 2008 financial crisis; Attorney General Jeff Sessions lifted the Obama administration's ban on the transfer of some military-surplus items to domestic law enforcement, rescinding guidelines that were created in the wake of Ferguson to protect the public from law-enforcement misuse of military-grade weapons; the Trump administration released new guidelines that allow states to seek waivers to require Medicaid recipients to work—requirements that represent a throwback to rejected racial stereotypes. These are but a few examples. During our meeting, however, we spoke generally about the work we'd accomplished and our hopes for the future. President Obama then turned his attention to us and issued a challenge, saying, "Now, you guys—you've got to keep this going. A lot of the accomplishments we made were policy, not law. They can be reversed."

I asked good-naturedly, "And what role are you going to play on the other side?"

He looked at me and said, "I'm not worried about what I'm going to do. I'm worried about what you're going to do."

At his farewell speech, he sounded the same note when he told the country, "It falls to each of us to be those anxious, jealous guardians of our democracy; to embrace the joyous task we've been given to continually try to improve this great nation of ours. Because for all our outward differences, we all share the same proud title: Citizen. Ultimately, that's what our democracy demands. It needs you."

We girded ourselves. Even though it seemed like a storm was brewing, we told ourselves it wasn't going to be that bad. We, like the rest of the country, were willing to afford Trump the chance to prove himself, to be presidential. We didn't anticipate that children would be separated from their families and locked in cages, that citizens from seven Muslim-majority countries would be barred from entering this country, that the lackluster federal response to a global pandemic would literally endanger lives. We didn't foresee Trump's total disregard for the rule of law though his campaign sentiment "I could shoot someone on Fifth Avenue and not lose voters" was a harbinger. No, Trump would reveal these truths to the country himself.

Whatever fears I had during my last meeting with Obama were confirmed in my first—and only—meeting with Trump's Attorney General Jeff Sessions. The NAACP, the National Urban League, the National Action Network, and the Legal Defense Fund had collectively opposed the nomination of Jeff Sessions in large part because of his open hostility to the Voting Rights Act. Nonetheless, early on in his appointment, Sessions reached out to me by phone, and we talked. I realize he was trying to make small talk, but on our first call, Sessions mentioned that his in-laws lived the next town over from Newville, Alabama, the town where my mother was buried eight years ago. I found it a bit awkward to bring up my mother's death in casual conversation, though I appreciated his effort in trying to connect with me. Sessions soon cut to the chase: he wanted to meet with civil rights leaders and the Justice Department. And so, a few days later, I found myself sitting in the same room where Robert Kennedy had championed civil rights and where I had personally met with former Attorneys General Janet Reno, Eric Holder, and Loretta Lynch to discuss the same. I listened to Sessions explain in no uncertain terms that if we had any hope that the Trump administration was going to continue down the path of voter protection or police reform, we were mistaken. The administration was taking a different route. End of story. He did not bite his tongue. He did not mince his words. It was one of the more polite racist meetings I've attended.

I asked how the Trump administration was going to handle the Eric Garner case, and Sessions said he couldn't speak to it. (A year later, the Department of Justice declined to bring charges against Garner's killer, New York City Police Department Officer Daniel Pantaleo, under federal civil rights laws. Upon the recommendation of an administrative judge, Pantaleo was fired five years after Garner's death.) My colleagues and I left the White House feeling disheartened but also resolved: at least there was no equivocating. It was like going to the doctor's knowing something's wrong, and then having the doc diagnose a life-altering disease. You're not shocked per se. You leave the doctor's office feeling a sense of determination. You know you're going to have to deal with the situation one way or another.

After a perfunctory press conference, my colleagues and I rededicated ourselves to doing what we do best. For me, that meant doing direct-action work, and I set to work organizing the Ministers' March for Justice.

We got ready.

Ministers' March for Justice

On Monday, August 28, 2017, I led the Ministers' March for Justice in Washington, DC, and asked clergy members of all faiths to commit to shining a light on issues central to the social-justice agenda. I also asked for help in holding Attorney General Sessions accountable for all people's civil rights. I specifically wanted this march to be held by ministers because, historically speaking, it has largely been religious leaders who have been at the forefront of social justice and civil rights. This is especially true in the Black church, where religious leadership has often been intertwined with civil rights leadership; they complement and strengthen one another. Over the years, I've witnessed an erosion of this symbiotic relationship and felt that the march could help reaffirm our mutual goals. The date of the march was intentional as it was the fifty-fourth anniversary of the March on Washington in which Martin Luther King Jr. gave his "I Have a Dream" speech. Fifty-four years to the day, and we're still fighting the good fight for voting rights, health care, criminal-justice reform, and economic justice. Same priorities, different era.

Approximately three thousand leaders, along with some of their congregants, marched the 1.7-mile route from the Martin Luther King Jr. Memorial to the Justice Department. A rainbow of faiths participated—everyone from Protestant preachers and Jewish cantors to Catholic nuns and Black Baptists. While everyone assembled was already dedicated to the ideals of the march, there was an increased sense of urgency to our gathering because of the Unite the Right rally in Charlottesville, where white supremacists, neo-Nazis, and members of the far-right and alt-right clashed with counterprotesters to devastating effect: self-identified white supremacist James Alex Fields Jr. intentionally drove his car into a gathering of counterprotesters, killing Heather Heyer and injuring nineteen other people. On the day of the march, several speakers criticized the silence of some within their own ranks on the subject of white supremacy. Before leading the march through downtown Washington, I addressed the crowd, saying, "You're going to see the victims of Nazism, the victims of white supremacy, march today to the Justice Department." Reverend Jim Wallis, founder of the social-justice organization and magazine *Sojourners*, said that the demonstration was fundamentally theological because, in his words, "the soul of the nation and the integrity of faith" were at stake. Standing before the crowd, he said, "We have to preach from every pulpit in America that racism is America's original sin."

This notion—that racism is America's original sin—is one that, unfortunately, our country still hasn't fully recognized. But Wallis was right: since the country's inception, Americans' socioeconomic status has been determined by race. Back then, the top tier was white and male. Second tier: white women. Native Americans were expendable. Black people were property. That was the basis of this country. Since then, the country has merged into various renegotiations of that power structure. New power structures don't evolve naturally, however. The renegotiations were hard fought, following Frederick Douglass's dictum, "Power concedes nothing without a demand." The biggest war in this country was the Civil War, where the very battle for a new power structure was fought outright in bloodshed. Since then, we've mustered various civil rights and human rights movements to redress the imbalance of our founding. We've voted politicians in and out of power, searching for an alignment between our core beliefs, the political, and a sense of human decency. And yet, in spite of this progress and our many struggles, we—as a country—have never really had a proper come-to-Jesus moment about race. Obama's beer summit with Harvard professor Henry Louis Gates Jr. and Sgt. James Crowley doesn't count. It's possible that the wide-sweeping protests following George Floyd's death may be the moment we've been waiting for, but unless real legislative change is made—and our voices are heard in the voting booth—the moment will pass us by.

How else could we have a president in office whose criticism of the Charlottesville rally was to say, "We condemn in the strongest possible terms this egregious display of hatred, bigotry, and violence, on many sides. On many sides. It's been going on for a long time in our country. Not Donald Trump, not Barack Obama. This has been going on for a long, long time." To use the phrase *on many sides* is to equate the actions and mentality of one group with another, and in the case of racism, we know this isn't true: there's a big difference between the oppressor and the oppressed, intolerance and tolerance, and hate and love. Hatred, bigotry, and violence have been a part of this country since its founding, but these aren't the ideals of our country; these aren't characteristics to live up to but, instead, to dispel and to cast out. Trump's refusal to fully condemn hatred and domestic terrorism—because, let's be clear, any hate crime is a form of terrorism—spoke volumes. It was, to my mind, a defining moment in Trump's presidency—one among many.

We act as if the shootings in Charleston, South Carolina, El Paso, Texas, and Pittsburgh, Pennsylvania, are isolated incidents, committed by insane individuals. It may be that the acts are insane, but they certainly aren't isolated. Taken together, they speak to a web of hatred. With time, there's the possibility that those on the other side of this hatred may become just as vitriolic in their reactions. I see storm clouds on our horizon, but it's a weather system entirely of our own making. Let me be clear: I do not condone violence of any sort, but if we are to avert ourselves from this kind of catastrophic confrontation, we need to begin working together to undo all that has been brought to the fore. We must restore balance and decency to the state of democracy itself.

The white supremacists who gathered in Charlottesville were there to protest the removal of a statue of Confederate General Robert E. Lee. That the ghosts of white power can't even concede the symbolism of racism indicates a real sickness in this country. The roots of racism run deep; it's not enough to pull out a few weeds. The entire root system is rotten and must be extracted. Removing Confederate statues and other relics of that period is one way America can confront its ugly past. It can help loosen the rot, but it's not enough. To address something so widespread and systemic, we need government, business, law enforcement, and community stakeholders working together to bridge racial divides. The real glue that will keep our nation together, though, is the church and its faith leaders. But, listen: you don't have to be religious to recognize and embrace the values that speak to our common humanity. It's possible to engage your sense of activism and human decency simply because it's the right thing to do.

Bishop Washington:
Do the Right Thing

In the first decade of our nation, a former slave named Richard Allen found himself preaching to a growing community of brothers and sisters in Philadelphia. He eventually founded African Methodist Episcopal Church

(AME) in 1794 as one of the country's first places of worship for Blacks. Today, the Black church is a fixture— a culture unto itself—within American society. Over the years, it hasn't been all Scripture, fiery sermons, and soaring gospel music. Because the church stands at the center of the Black community, it's also been an essential bedrock for the civil rights movement and activism. In fact, it was my faith that led me to the world of politics. Or rather, it was my parents' fascination with a Pentecostal minister named Bishop Frederick Douglas Washington that led me to church, and then he gave me the foundation for the rest of my life.

Bishop Washington was the minister of a church in Montclair, New Jersey, before moving to Brooklyn with his wife, Madame Ernestine Beatrice Washington. In Brooklyn, the couple began old-fashioned summer revival meetings, setting up church under an old tent with sawdust for its carpet. His revivals caught on. Everyone was curious about what went on under that great tent. On mornings when Bishop Washington preached, the tent was filled to capacity; no one seemed to mind crowding in, even when it was a hot summer day. Neighbors, family, and friends went to the tent to visit with one another, share the local gossip, and get their dose of God's Word. My parents started attending the revivals, too. It didn't take long before they formally joined Bishop Washington's church. The congregation grew in number until the minister was able to purchase the old Loew's Bedford Theatre at 1372 Bedford Avenue in Bedford-Stuyvesant, which he turned into the Washington Temple Church of God in Christ. I was baptized in that church and grew up emulating Bishop Washington's sermons in the bathroom mirror of my childhood home.

When I was four years old, the church created an anniversary program to honor the kids who served on the Junior Usher Board. Every child was encouraged to participate by singing or performing, reading a poem, that sort of thing. I said I wanted to preach. The kids started to laugh. Hazel Griffin, the program's supervisor, said, "Don't laugh. God can call boy preachers."

On July 9, 1959, I delivered my first sermon to the congregation. I stood on a box at the pulpit because I was too short to be seen over the lectern otherwise. For my first sermon, I chose John 14:1, "Let not your heart be troubled: ye believe in God, believe also in me." Because I was still too young to read, I delivered the sermon from memory, serving up Bishop Washington's words mixed in with some of my own. I concluded with the last verse: "But that the world may know that I love the Father; and as the Father gave me commandment, even as I do." I felt especially preacher-like when I said, "Arise, let us go hence." Bishop Washington later ordained and licensed me as a minister when I was nine years old. Besides supporting me in my pursuits to become a preacher, he also encouraged me to join the God-directed civil rights movement when I was a teenager.

By my teenage years, my father had already abandoned our family. He'd left my mother, my sister, and me to start a new family with his stepdaughter. My mother, newly single, faced the daunting challenge of raising two children alone. My dad had always had the latest Cadillac, but with him gone, we adjusted to new circumstances in Brownsville, Brooklyn, a neighborhood later known as Mike Tyson's stomping grounds. During the 1960s, the area became largely Black. (It had previously been a mix of Jewish and Black.) With unemployment at 17 percent—twice the city's as a whole—there was little in the way of community institutions or economic opportunities. There was no middle class, and residents didn't own the businesses upon which they relied. Having the orations of social justice from church in my ear while also seeing, living, and breathing the social injustice of life in Brownsville set my course: I decided that my ministry was going to be one of social justice. The intersection between the political and the religious spoke to me. I set about studying the careers of men like Adam Clayton Powell Jr., Reverend William Jones, and other leaders, including Reverend Jesse Jackson, and concluded that you couldn't be sincerely religious without also actualizing your faith in the political landscape, at least not in the Black church.

Bishop Washington was somewhat civic-minded. He came up during the Great Migration, which informed his politics. In many respects, he was the embodiment of that era, a time when Blacks were shifting away from the old Southern way of life and forging new paths in the North. He straddled both sides, and his life was spent testing out the differences. He'd grown up in the deep South in Little Rock, Arkansas, during Jim Crow. At the time, Southern Blacks belonged to the party of Lincoln, but as they migrated to the North, Midwest, and West, their party affiliation began to shift Democratic. The 1932 election of Roosevelt marked the beginning of the change. By 1948, Truman won 77 percent of the Black vote; it helped that he ordered the desegregation of armed services and signed an executive order that set up regulations against racial bias in federal employment. Lyndon B. Johnson pushed through the Civil Rights Act of 1964 and got 94 percent of the Black vote. By 1970, the South was home to less than half of the country's Black population, and most Blacks identified as Democrats.

I remember Governor Rockefeller and Jackie Robinson, Republicans both, used to come to Bishop Washington's church. The minister welcomed both parties, but as the civil rights movement gathered momentum, he was cautioned by his Republican friends not to get too involved. He was named after the famous civil rights leader Frederick Douglass, though, so you know he had to live up to his name. Bishop Washington weighed their caution against the oppression he saw around him and had experienced himself both in the South and the North. Despite pressure from his Republican congregants, Bishop Washington made the choice, at great personal cost, to invite the Freedom Riders and Martin Luther King Jr. to speak at his church. In fact, the first time I saw Martin Luther King Jr. was at that church. Unfortunately, by the time I came up in the civil rights movement, King was already dead. (I was thirteen years old on April 4, 1968, the day he was assassinated while standing on the second-story balcony of the Lorraine Motel in Memphis, Tennessee.) When Bishop Washington opened his church to those civil rights leaders, he helped set in motion a movement that would forever link the church with direct-action social justice. Just by opening his door, he helped carry a torch through it.

Bishop Washington lived a good long life, and he and I spoke frequently. In his later years, we often talked about how he came to decide to align the church with the civil rights movement—the religion with the political—and keep his rapport with his Republican congregants. He explained, "Sometimes you have to make a hard choice."

I asked, "How do you make your decision?"

He answered, "By understanding it isn't difficult to do the right thing." His Republican congregants and friends may not have agreed with what he did, but they understood it. I believe the human spirit recognizes when a man stands for something. The Holy Spirit does, too.

Woe to Those Who Put Bitter to Sweet

It's dispiriting to think how Bishop Washington's words would fall on deaf ears today. When faith is used as a political weapon, we're no better than Herod or the modern-day equivalent of a despot. During his 2016 campaign run, it was questionable whether Trump, who had been married three times and wasn't known for his religious conviction, would attract the votes of the white Evangelical. At the voting booth, however, the white Evangelicals showed up. According to data from the Pew Research Center, eight in ten self-identified, white, born-again/Evangelical Christians voted for Trump. This 65 percentage–point margin of victory matched or exceeded the victory margin for George W. Bush in 2004, John McCain in 2008, and Mitt Romney in 2012. How do Evangelicals justify voting for a man whose ethics and morals don't correspond with their faith in the most basic way? The Evangelical faith, much like that of the Black church, has historically struggled with entrenched sexism, and a vote for Trump, in this respect, may have simply been a vote against Hillary Clinton, but this anecdotal insight doesn't explain the

Evangelicals' continued support for the president when his lack of moral judgment brought about an impeachment nor when his administration caged refugee children at our Southern border nor, in the midst of a pandemic, when he vaguely suggested that our economy is more important than the lives of our grandparents. Never mind Trump's track history with women or the vulgar language he uses to objectify them.

I applauded Mark Galli, the editor-in-chief of *Christianity Today*, when he penned a moving piece in the magazine that called for Trump's removal from office during impeachment. He wrote: "The facts in this instance are unambiguous: the president of the United States attempted to use his political power to coerce a foreign leader to harass and discredit one of the president's political opponents. This is not only a violation of the Constitution; more importantly, it is profoundly immoral." Galli went on to describe Trump as "a near perfect example of a human being who is morally lost and confused." What does it say, then, about those who follow him?

Historically speaking, it's antithetical for most religious leaders to weigh in on politics, and for good reason: any congregation comprises both Republicans and Democrats. But we are not in ordinary times. Instead, the very ethics of our religious foundations are being tested and weaponized by the most powerful in political office. This couldn't be more apparent than when Trump's team allowed the dispersion of groups of people protesting police brutality at Lafayette Square with flash grenades and gas so Trump could amble across the street for a photo-op in front of St. John's Episcopal Church. Do we stay true to ourselves and do the right thing, or do we let ourselves be led astray by the cruelty of Trump's politics? If you choose to be led astray, then accept the fact that you are no longer a man or woman of the Christian faith. You are part of a Christian right that is not right Christians. For the rest of my conservative Evangelical brothers and sisters, I issue a challenge: don't become Democrat. Become Christian.

Creature Comforts

Though I started my life in the Pentecostal church, I was baptized a second time as an adult in the Baptist church. Ironically, Bishop Washington introduced me to the man who would perform that second baptism: Reverend William Jones. I met Reverend Jones when I was still a young boy. With my father gone, both Bishop Washington and my mother saw that I needed some guidance, especially since some of the boys my age were beginning to follow a more militant form of Black-rights justice. That wasn't the route of a boy preacher.

Reverend Jones was a lion in New York City's Black church and community. He was in a league of his own. Even as a young man, I could see that. Impeccably dressed in a suit and tie and well-educated with degrees from the University of Kentucky and Crozer Theological Seminary—the same school Martin Luther King Jr. attended—he could have followed in the footsteps of his grandfather and father, both of whom were respected Baptist preachers. Jones, however, wasn't interested in that kind of life. He was after something bigger. He was someone Jesse Jackson called a *tree-shaker*, a person who wanted to speak truth to power and incite real change. I learned about activism from Jones. In fact, the first time I was arrested for protesting, I was with him.

Over the years, civil rights leaders have traded information and direct-action tactics with one another, honing what works and discarding what doesn't. Jones learned from men like Leon Sullivan, who had perfected the art of the boycott in Philadelphia, and his friend and colleague Martin Luther King Jr. who, in turn, had adopted Gandhi's nonviolent practices for his own. When I started my own youth organization, I turned to Jones for advice on how to organize and run my demonstrations and protests. It pains me to admit that I had to suffer a few knocks of my own before taking his words to heart. His advice, however, was prescient and can be distilled into three points: 1) Do your research. No one should know your business or what you're trying to accomplish better than you. 2) Remain nonviolent at all times. If given the chance, the opposition will say that, by your very nature of being Black, you're not worthy of whatever it is you're demanding. Don't live up to the image of violence they want to project. 3) Never get more caught up in the drama than what you're using the drama to achieve. It took years for me to faithfully apply the wisdom of that last tenet, but in fairness to another mentor of mine, Jesse Jackson, who Jones introduced me to, sometimes a little drama goes a long way, especially in New York City.

Reverend Jones had an outsized impact on my life. He was a scholar and a theologian in the tradition of Martin Luther King Jr. Both men were academic by nature. Martin Luther King Jr., according to his wife, Coretta, was always reading several books at the same time. Jones lived on President Street in Crown Heights, Brooklyn, on a stretch known as Preacher's Row on account of it also being home to Reverend Bishop and Reverend Dr. Gardner Taylor, the so-called dean of American preaching. As if it weren't enough to be in a neighborhood full of preachers, Jones had also come from a long line of preachers; he was truly immersed in the faith. I once asked him why he hadn't followed in the footsteps of his father, forsaking the civil rights movement to become the leader of a big-time church, with all the adulation that implies. His answer was firm. "There's a difference between your career and your calling, Al," he said. "Don't get so comfortable with the creature comforts that you forget why you came to the faith in the first place." While I came from the streets and may have worked my way up to the suites, I know better than most that penthouse talk and creature comforts don't help those of us still in the basement. Faith not only helps keep me grounded in my calling, it also sets my moral compass true.

I still use many of the tactics and practices developed by the first wave of civil rights leaders. Jones met with leaders and members of the community and church every Saturday morning in the basement at Brooklyn's Bethany Baptist Church. The meeting was a kind of open forum where people could voice everything from the local to the national and find camaraderie and kindred spirits. Jesse Jackson did the same thing in Chicago. It's a tradition I've upheld as well: every Saturday morning for the past twenty-eight years, I've hosted the action rally that's broadcast live from NAN's Harlem headquarters. I accept calls into my daily radio show and field questions and comments on everything from Kobe Bryant's death to how to file for unemployment insurance. Part of the strategy for meeting on Saturday mornings is to mobilize possible protesters for any direct-action campaigns, demonstrations, or social service work immediately afterward. During the COVID-19 outbreak, for example, the radio show became a megaphone, and we used it to spread the word that NAN had partnered with the World Central Kitchen. Afterward, we transformed the headquarters into a food-distribution center and, in the first day of its opening, provided five hundred prepackaged hot and cold meals to those Harlem residents in need.

In addition to this Saturday-morning session, I also host a weekly radio show, *Keepin' It Real*, Monday through Friday. The calls are from everyday people: the grandmother in Harlem who can't afford to pay her electricity bill, the young mother in Chicago who doesn't know how to report police harassment of her teenage sons. The Black community relies on my radio show and NAN because they don't know where else to turn. They call NAN because their trust in public institutions, their elected officials, and other so-called experts is so badly eroded it's practically nonexistent. The sad truth is, if the need didn't exist, neither would we. But it does, and we do. If we couldn't help answer that need, people would stop calling. But the phones keep ringing. We can put pressure on an elected official to address a particular issue, and more often than not, that pressure helps move the dial. National Action Network represents the voice of many, and as any elected official knows, if he or she gets a call from us, it's because that voice has been raised to a scream.

This is deeply personal for me. The mother who calls in to ask for help in keeping on her electric could have been my mother. The young man found dead in the street could have been me. These people aren't strangers to me. I know what it feels like to not be able to make ends meet, to feel the threat of eviction. It wasn't so long ago that I was the guy who wrote out a check and hoped I'd get enough money in the black to cover it before it bounced. When I get a call from a fearful mother, I don't see her in terms of being a stat. She is as real to me as the flesh and blood of my own family.

Besides my radio show, I also host *PoliticsNation* as well as make other regular television appearances. All told, I do a combined seventeen hours of radio and television media on any given week. The difference between the conversations that take place in the television studio—the suites—and the radio station—the streets—is staggering. Television is littered with experts of all kinds, people like senators and congressmen, journalists and talking heads, all of whom are encouraged to give their supposedly informed opinion on a variety of subjects.

The calls I get on my radio show, however, are from average Americans living their lives and feeling the repercussions of the experts' televised opinions on a daily basis. I often experience something like whiplash several times a day: How is it possible that the conversations the experts entertain are completely different than those that move the people on the ground?

There are those who believe change can come from within the system, from the people in the board meetings. I've never had much luck with that. I've found that the more powerful the person, the higher up they are in the chain, the more they want to keep things quiet lest they lose the power that got them to that position in the first place. Of course, there are a few exceptions to that general rule, Obama being one of them. I've made peace with the fact that my strength lies in championing and organizing activism on the ground. I may not be an insider, but I'm working hard on the outside to make sure that the insiders can move toward power and, with that power, help lift everyone else, too. The other side—insider or outsider—can't open doors on their own. In this respect, Barack Obama and I understood our roles with each other perfectly.

As Jesus said to his disciples in Luke 9:23, "If any man will come after me, let him deny himself, and take up his cross daily, and follow me." Whenever you raise uncomfortable truths, it's a burden. If you're not willing to bear the cross, then fine, don't join me on the path of justice. Surprisingly, though, the more you carry the cross and work toward justice, the stronger you become until you don't notice the burden anymore. Your strength comes to define you—and not the cross itself. In my experience, it's always been the people on the ground—those average, everyday Americans—who reach critical mass, pick up their crosses, and change the conversation.

When Reverend Abernathy picked up the cross of the civil

rights movement after Martin Luther King Jr.'s death, many questioned if he was going to be able to fill King's shoes. He often had a retort at the ready: "Maybe I can't fill Dr. King's shoes. But I've got some sandals of my own." It's a funny and disarming statement, but it also speaks to a greater wisdom. You've got to be as real on the inside as you are on the outside. And at the end of the day, you've got to be your own person, with a set of values stronger than any temptation of creature comforts. In order to incite real change, however, you need to be something more: a tree-shaker.

TREE-SHAKERS AND JELLY-MAKERS

When Jesse Jackson ran for the Democratic presidential nomination in 1988 and won seven million votes, he could have parlayed his popularity and experience into becoming part of the Democratic hierarchy. Instead, he went back to Chicago and worked on building up the National Rainbow Coalition, which merged with People United to Save Humanity (PUSH) in 1996. I once asked him why he went back to Chicago when he could have run for any other office. He told me, "Homeboy, we're not built for that world. We've got to keep the movement going, the movement Martin Luther King Jr. started. There are tree-shakers in this world, and there are jelly-makers. You and I are tree-shakers. We know how to shake things up. But we'll never be able to stop and pick the fruit and taste the jam. We won't get to taste a lot of sweetness in this world but we'll shake a lot of trees." Years later, I had the opportunity to interview Makaziwe Mandela-Amuah, one of Nelson Mandela's daughters, who told me that Mandela's given name at birth by his father was Rolihlahla. In Xhosa, one of the official languages of South Africa, Rolihlahla means *pulling the branch of a tree* or, more commonly, *a troublemaker.* It would seem that us troublemakers have a shared history of taking down trees all around the world.

Jesse, like a lot of the early civil rights leaders, was originally from the South, and he honed what he learned there and brought that knowledge north. I think most people today don't understand the choices that the Black community had to make during the 1960s while living in the South. Back then, it was more convenient and safer to go along to get along. In some parts of the country, this thinking still applies. But there were those among us, like Bishop Washington and my mother and father, and the millions of other Blacks who migrated north, who didn't want to be subjugated to Jim Crow, who were done with going along to get along. The North held the promise of freedom, economic and otherwise. By 1916, an industrialized job in the North paid three times more than what Blacks could make working the land in the rural South. The 1910s through the mid-1930s saw the rise of the Harlem Renaissance, a golden age in Black culture where Black art, literature, and entertainment flourished, and where Northern social and political issues found its pulse.

There was racism in the North, too, and in some ways, it was more insidious. In the North, Blacks weren't told they couldn't work at a particular store or company, they just weren't hired. Or they were hired but at a reduced rate and with no promise of promotion. I'm one of the few civil rights leaders to be born in the North; I came up in New York City. Whereas racism in the South was blatant—KKK rallies and lynchings, Jim Crow and segregation—it was institutionalized in the North. In the South, racism was a knife in your side. In the North, it's a thorn. You have to pull it out. I've had to show the thorn to people, especially white folk, over and over again, first to let them know it's real because, to them, it isn't obvious that it even exists. Second, because it's still there—smaller, yes, but it hurts even today.

It's one of the reasons my style was initially so caustic. To point something out that's been hidden—and wants to *remain* hidden as part of the protected status quo—you have no choice but to be confrontational. My mother's generation, and the generations before her, understood the racism they ran from in the South, and they understood the unfairness and the racism that they ran into in the North. In their hearts, my mother, Bishop Washington, and Jesse Jackson knew I was right to call out the racial injustices of the North, but in their minds, they just hoped I wouldn't get killed doing it. Not everyone wanted me to point out the racism of the North. Some of the church's more fundamentalist members weren't pleased I was out there in the world, calling out injustices from the mountaintop. But Bishop Washington always stood by me.

When I marched to protest Michael Griffith's murder in Howard Beach, Bishop Washington let me hold a rally at Washington Temple. Hosea Williams, one of Martin Luther King Jr.'s most trusted lieutenants, spoke at that rally and presented me with an award. Williams gave these awards to anyone he felt was keeping the Martin Luther King Jr. movement alive. The media often wrote about my tracksuits and my showman's hair, my habit of wearing a flashy medallion. What they failed to realize was that the medallion I wore around my neck was the award I received from Hosea Williams, and I wore it with pride. You couldn't pay me to take it off.

STAY ON THE ONE

One night in the early 1970s, James Brown and I were driving around in Augusta, Georgia, as we'd done on so many other nights, him talking and me, a teenage boy, listening rapt with attention. Suddenly, Mr. Brown swung the van off the side of the road. Across the street was the United House of Prayer for All People, the Augusta chapter of Daddy Grace, a charismatic Black evangelist famously known as one of the first religious Black leaders who put a band in church.

"You hear that band?" he asked, and I strained my ears, listening closely. I picked up the distant sound of church music, the call and response of the choir. Mr. Brown went on to tell me that as a young boy, he'd often stood outside that very church and listened to the music. He'd grown up poor, and it showed in his clothing and his appearance. He never went inside, and no one ever invited him in. I imagined him as a young boy, cast out and hungry, yet feeding his soul with the sound of music.

"Listen to the drumbeat," he said. Mr. Brown went on to explain that what I heard was the half-beat, a sound unique to the drummer of Daddy Grace's band but one that Mr. Brown would go on to popularize as the sound of soul music. "Stay on the one," he said, and I smiled. By emphasizing the first beat in the 4/4 time, he shifted the rhythm of soul and funk music.

Years later, Mr. Brown offered me the opportunity of a lifetime: he invited me to join him on the road. Having already spent some time off and on as a guest on the road with him, I knew what that gig would entail: long nights, lots of traveling, and a roving cast of characters, celebrities, and flashy marquee signs. Without realizing it, when Mr. Brown made me that offer, he blessed me with one of the most defining crossroads of my life: Would I choose a life of fame and celebrity or one of social justice?

As I weighed the two paths before me—fame or activism—I decided to put my fate in God's hands. I relied on my faith when I made the decision to continue my path as an activist.

I didn't have any blueprint. I didn't have a plan. What I had was an unshakable belief that I had to do God's work, and what is God's work if it isn't activism? How could I possibly be at peace with myself or preach the lessons of the Bible to a congregation without being an embodiment of those lessons myself? People often find faith when they're at their most compromised, when things have fallen apart. Why? Because when you have nothing—when you're a poor Black boy living in Augusta, Georgia, or a white boy living in a trailer in the backwoods of Topeka, Kansas—you have nothing to lose, and faith becomes your anchor. Faith offers comfort when there's none to be found in your community. Let's be clear, however: the economic decisions, government regulations, and zoning laws that put so much of this country at a disadvantage aren't arbitrary. They are very much the product of a well-calculated plan and strategy, a scheme, to keep the wealthy and the privileged at a unique advantage. Suffering can be manufactured. There's nothing wrong with that boy in Augusta or that boy in Topeka; there's something wrong with our society.

Faith has been an operating principle my entire life. It's the intangible—the belief in something even if you can't see it. It's not the end of a well-calculated plan or strategy, though faith may help you make the moral decisions that further shape a plan. It's conviction. It's belief in the greater good in both yourself and in others. For some, like James Brown, faith is the space between the beats when anything can happen. He found his faith in the half-beat. I found mine in the work.

No Justice, No Peace

I started the National Action Network in 1991 because I didn't see a faith-based direct-action organization in the North the way that Martin Luther King Jr. had organized his movement in the South. I also didn't see anyone dealing with the real pain and problems of people in the streets. I intentionally based our headquarters in Harlem. Over the years, our headquarters have hosted an array of high-profile speakers, politicians, and public figures—everyone from Bill Clinton and Kamala Harris to Sean Hannity. I felt it was important, when dealing with high-profile personalities such as these men and women, that they come to us. Politicians and pundits should have to explain the rationale behind stop-and-frisk policies, criminal-justice reform, and zoning laws to the demographic that feels the on-the-ground effects of such discriminatory legislation. Beyond this, I wanted the little Black boys and girls sitting in the back of the room to know that the former president of the United States or perhaps the future president was there to speak to them, and that what they said would be held accountable. After all, senators and congressmen and the president work on behalf of these children and their families. Their dreams and fears aren't something to be cast aside. Instead, they inform the work of these men and women and are the reason, I hope, that some became politicians in the first place. It's important for these boys and girls to see former mayor Michael Bloomberg or Senator Sanders on 145th Street if for no other reason than it validates their worth.

The road to the White House passes through the home of the Black family. There's no getting around this fact. Politicians are either on the right side or the wrong side of that road. It's become a political rite of passage for candidates to come to Harlem and address the Black constituency on their terms. If a politician is with me, we're either having soul food at Sylvia's or talking policy at NAN headquarters. But here's the thing: the road to the White House doesn't start or end in Harlem. It also passes through the rural farmlands of Kentucky and the manufacturing plants of the rust belt, which is why the

Democrats—progressive and centrist alike—would be wise to stage a few of their own rallies and meet-and-greets there. Trump doesn't hold a monopoly on the plights of these communities. It's important to reach out, to make the attempt to bridge the gaps and heal the wounds of this country. When one community hurts, chances are others are hurting, too.

Years ago, in Borough Park, Brooklyn, four officers of the New York City Police Department killed a Breslover Hasid man named Gidone Busch. Though my staff was sensitive to the situation and didn't want to inflame the Jewish community, NAN reached out to the grieving family, and I went to them. Why? Because I've been comforting grieving families for decades, and the grief this family felt was no different from the pain endured by that of a Black family who's suffered the same. Unfortunately, a tragedy such as this speaks to the overriding need for better policing legislation no matter the neighborhood; it transcends racial boundaries. Moments like this define our worth. Even at the risk of being rejected, it's important that we still reach out to each other. Doing so not only affirms our character, it also speaks volumes about what we value most in this society. I'd rather attempt and fail than fail to attempt.

Today, NAN has over 106 chapters nationwide, and we partner with several local organizations and communities to promote a modern civil rights agenda that includes the fight for one standard of justice, decency, and equal opportunities for all people regardless of race, religion, ethnicity, citizenship, criminal record, economic status, gender, gender expression, or sexuality. We welcome everyone to the table. Our initiatives include criminal-justice reform, police accountability, crisis intake and victim assistance, voting rights, corporate responsibility, and pension diversity. We also have a youth leadership program for ages eleven to twenty-five. I've personally been working at the forefront of our social-justice agenda, leading many of these initiatives for decades. We've come a long way, but there's still much to do, especially in the area of civil rights under the Trump administration.

OUR FIGHT

A few years ago, I was the guest speaker at a prestigious university. Afterward, a man from the audience approached me and said, "When I was younger, there was a Black mayor in every major city—Atlanta, Los Angeles, Chicago, New York—at the same time. What happened?"

I said, "You grew up taking that progress for granted. I grew up during a time when we fought to get David Dinkins to become mayor. We fought for Tom Bradley, Harold Washington, and Maynard Jackson." I can't lay the blame entirely at the younger generation's feet. Far from it. The older generation has made some missteps. Perhaps in our efforts to shield our sons and daughters from some of the brutality we faced ourselves, we didn't sit them down and tell them that the fight wasn't over. I didn't want my daughters to spend a night in jail fighting for their rights. I myself had spent far too many nights in a cell because I'd done exactly that. Perhaps my daughters could be spared. The problem is, once you start protecting the younger generations like that, you don't prepare them. The other generational problem we have is cultural: my so-called old-school form of activism doesn't impress some of the younger activists, and I get that. They want to claim their own. But our differences in style shouldn't account for us not being able to work together. I use the techniques I do because they're tried and true; they work. That said, I'm not against other models of activism if they work, too. Different paths lead to the same summit. If the old school and the new school are separated by the opposition, there's no continuity of struggle, and without continuity, without the wisdom of lessons learned, we're at a strategic disadvantage.

When Obama became president, we let ourselves get fat: we had a Black president, a Black *family* in the White House. I will never forget when I went to Ferguson, Missouri, two days after Michael Brown's fatal shooting. The city was in the midst of riots and deep unrest. I encouraged the activists on the ground to work respectfully with the authorities. A young man told me he wanted to but couldn't because he didn't trust The Man. I looked at him and asked, "Do you know who our attorney general is?" He looked at me blankly, and I answered my own question: "Eric Holder. We *are* The Man." Not only did we have a Black president, but we also had a Black man as the head of law enforcement in our country, who was succeeded by a Black woman, Loretta Lynch. So many of us kicked back and relaxed. We let President Obama carry the mantle of the Black experience without realizing that much of the change he presided over was policy and not legislation. We felt the cultural shift of what it meant to have a Black president—it was empowering, emboldening, and it was about time. Some of us stopped fighting, eager to enjoy the gains we had secured. Eight years later, the backlash has reminded us of why we got in the fight in the first place. Today's generation may not know the civil rights struggle or what it meant to be beaten down trying to vote or to be a grown man and still called a boy. But they know Michael Brown and Eric Garner. They know Ahmaud Arbery. They know their uncle or husband or brother who's in jail. They know Colin Kaepernick can't get a job because he took a knee to protest police brutality. So, we're invested in the same fight after all; it's just a new year. Black unemployment, criminal-justice reform, police brutality, and voter suppression remain still some of the most pressing issues facing the Black community.

Black Unemployment

Prior to mass unemployment caused by the COVID-19 crisis, the rates for Black unemployment had fallen to 6.8 nationally, a historically low percentage, and one that President Trump touted at any majority-Black event. It's worth pointing out, however, that Trump never intentionally targeted the Black unemployment rate as something he wanted to address; it was an incidental side effect of economic recovery, which was happening long before he got into office.

Valerie Wilson, director for the Economic Policy Institute, attributes the improvement to the prolonged strength of the US labor market. Unemployment numbers for Blacks have fallen consistently for the past several years: when Trump entered the White House, the rate was already at 7.8 percent. In June of 2019, it was 6.4 percent. The unemployment rate among Blacks and Latinos is still higher than white unemployment and doesn't account for the incarceration rates among these populations. When the unemployment numbers are adjusted to account for the incarceration rates and the employment-to-population ratio, the racial gap looks more like a chasm, especially when you consider Trump's attempts to pass legislation and a budget that's particularly damaging to economically vulnerable workers. It doesn't matter if the Black unemployment rate is low if the country's tax policy and health care programs only help wealthier, white Americans. It doesn't matter if the Black unemployment rate is low if Trump equivocated on Charlottesville. It doesn't matter if the Black unemployment rate is low if Trump decries immigrants from "shithole countries" in reference to Haiti and Africa but lauds those from Norway. Make no mistake: these are intentional comments with intentional consequences. The falling Black unemployment rate was incidental and doesn't begin to take into account the full details of the Black experience.

When they are employed, Black workers with a college or advanced degree are more likely than their white counterparts to be underemployed when it comes to their skill level—about 40 percent in a job that doesn't require a college degree compared with 31 percent of white college grads. This difference is historical and institutional. It isn't a reflection of merit. We had different starting points: the white worker has decades of advantages built in his favor, while the Black worker often starts from a place of systemic disadvantage. Institutionalized racism is pervasive as former mayor Michael Bloomberg noted in a speech he delivered in Tulsa, Oklahoma, to commemorate the 1921 race riots there. Bloomberg said, "Where slavery ended, systemic bias quickly took its place... The typical Black household remains almost ten times poorer than the typical white household." Bloomberg himself acknowledged his own wealth and privilege, knowing that his "story might have turned our very differently if I had been Black, and that more Black Americans of my generation would have ended up with far more wealth had they been white." Even when a tighter labor market has helped to reduce the overall Black employment rate, it hasn't been enough to erase racial inequality.

Whatever recent employment gains have been made by the Black community will most likely be erased by the pandemic. In March 2020, over three million unemployment claims were filed—millions more than the number of people who filed during the 2008 recession. The Federal Reserve slashed its benchmark interest rate by a full percentage point to near 0 to help support the economy, which will undoubtedly and disproportionately impact minorities, historically low-income earners. During the last recession, minority groups struggled the most and were hardest hit. If history repeats itself—and it looks like it will—these same groups will see their gains disappear.

Criminal-Justice Reform

Our penal system is staggering: as of 2018, 698 per 100,000 people are in prison, and a disproportionate number of those who are incarcerated are people of color. Today, roughly 2.2 million people are imprisoned, a sevenfold increase in incarceration from approximately 300,000 people in 1970. In 2010, one in ten Black men between the ages of twenty and forty were incarcerated—approximately ten times that of their white peers. Incarceration has been swelling each year. Prisons just keep getting bigger and bigger. With operational costs of approximately $80 billion a year, big prisons are big business, too.

Studies have shown that, over the years, the incarceration rate has risen independent of crime but not of criminal-justice policy. If mass incarceration showed that crime actually declined, that would be one thing. But it hasn't. Unfortunately, all mass incarceration has done is create a cycle of dependence and dysfunction and increased the suffering in Black families. Among all Black males born since the late 1970s, one in four went to prison by their midthirties; among high-school dropouts, seven in ten went to prison. Think of what this does to the Black family, to the wives and girlfriends and children left behind.

Time and time again, we've seen legislation, like stop-and-frisk, disproportionately target people of color. When I started fighting racial profiling, I focused my attention on the so-called Gold Coast of New Jersey, where wealthy Black athletes, lawyers, and entertainers kept getting pulled over on 95 South. Their wealth made them suspect to their white neighbors—"Where'd you get that Mercedes?"

"Where are you coming from?"

"Who invited you?" Of course, the courts later proved that Blacks were being stopped disproportionately on that portion of the highway.

When the biggest building in your neighborhood is the prison, it informs who you become, white or Black. Most of our prisons today function as social service programs, providing health care, meals, and shelter for populations with historic unemployment rates, and employing the working poor to maintain its model of big business. The one thing, it seems, the prisons don't provide in any real or comprehensive way is rehabilitation. There are some individuals who are beyond rehab, but most are not. We need to refocus our attention on helping to rehabilitate the criminal. When I was growing up, detention centers used to be called correction facilities, the connotation being *we can correct you.* The spirit of a correction facility was to provide training, therapy, and programs that helped address problematic behavior as well as to reintroduce and acclimate the individual to society. Today, the kind of training going on in most jails is hardened criminals teaching petty criminals how to step up their game.

To say someone is incapable of reform is to imply that he is also incapable of that most basic of human skills: thought. It's implied that a person who cannot think is also incapable of exercising judgment or making choices and is, therefore, less than human. We dehumanize the criminal so as to avoid our collective shame about our failure to provide truly adequate programs, medical care, and therapy to those behind bars. We say they don't deserve the help or a warm bed or the opportunity to reform. And what does that make us? Jesus didn't help those who didn't need it. He served the lepers, the sinners, and the outcasts. What kind of nation makes a profit in locking up people? Who will be an advocate for the prisoner?

In the spirit of unity, in March 2020, I made a moral appeal to the White House and President Trump during the outbreak of COVID-19, asking him to consider the homeless and the incarcerated. To my surprise, Trump called me back. It was the first time he and I had spoken since his election win. I respectfully asked that we be sensitive to the fact that these populations must be tested and cared for, not only because to do so is a humanitarian imperative but also because containment of the virus is vital. We cannot tell the homeless to stay at home when they don't have one, or the prisoners to practice social distancing when they are in close range to one another most of the time. Testing becomes even more important in these populations. Trump said he would consider my plea and would look into the situation with no commitment. After our call, I got on the line with other civil rights leaders and organizations like Marc Morial, president of the National Urban League; Derrick Johnson, president of the NAACP; Sherrilyn Ifill, president and director-counsel of the NAACP Legal Defense and Educational Fund; and Melanie Campbell, president of the Black Women's Roundtable, along with Senator Chuck Schumer and Speaker of the House Nancy Pelosi to mobilize our efforts in this area. Criminal-justice reform must be above partisan politics.

Police Brutality

No one knows how many people police kill every year. *The Washington Post*'s Fatal Force database attempts to track the numbers, but even its stats are incomplete. It doesn't record the number of deaths in police custody or as the result of beatings. It doesn't include the number of deaths from people who were killed by off-duty cops. Law-enforcement agencies, politicians, lobbyists, and the NRA purposely withhold data from government agencies. According to Fatal Force, 1,004 people were shot and killed by police in 2019. How many were killed with a choke hold or with a knee to their neck? Here's what I know: I know that I have visited far too many morgues, funeral homes, and cemeteries in my lifetime. I've seen too many Black boys and men cut down. I know that no matter how eloquent my eulogy, nothing will bring these men back to their women and children, their family.

In 2018, I went to Sacramento, California, to speak at Stephon Clark's funeral. Clark was a twenty-two-year-old student, shot dead in the backyard of his grandmother's house by two police officers. When I stepped away from the podium, I was emotionally exhausted. A few days later, I was speaking with a friend of mine, Reverend K. W. Tulloss, who asked, "You still get emotional at these things?" I responded, "When you stop feeling, it's time to get out of the work of civil rights. When it stops being personal, it becomes professional, and you're not really an activist anymore." My sense of anger at the injustice I've seen and still witness along with my passion for change motivate me and help keep my nose to the grindstone. I willingly engage myself with the pain and suffering not because I'm a preacher, although it is my religious duty to care for and protect my congregants. I engage myself because I refuse to be afraid in the face of wickedness and hatred. The moment you allow hatred to prosper, accept it as part of the status quo, something to be normalized, then you've relegated yourself to the status of being a second-class citizen, and that is something I refuse to do.

I often accompany family members to identify the body of their loved one. I do this in my capacity as a preacher and to help give fortitude. Despite having made this journey more times than I can count, it's not something I do easily. It's hard, lonely, emotional work. I don't care if it was the first time I accompanied a family or if it was last week, it always turns me inside out because when I look at these boys, these young men cut down, I think, *That could be my grandson. That could be me.* Every Black man knows this feeling; you grow up with it. It becomes not just a part of your thinking but thought itself, something you contend with every minute of every day. Much of the counseling and the strategic, calm advice I give the grieving families I have to remind myself, because it stirs up a deep anger inside. There's nothing that can describe looking at the dead body of a boy who did nothing wrong. Worse, that the very people he trusted—officers entrusted by law to protect and serve their community—killed him. I have to channel that anger into a passion for change, into energy to keep doing what I do, into getting you to rise up with me to march and get organized and say this has to stop.

When a grieving family calls me, the first questions I ask are, "How are you with rent? How are you going to pay for the funeral? Which family member is ostracized and not speaking with the rest of the family?" I ask these kinds of questions because I know that most people are barely scraping by. I ask because I know that every family has skeletons in the closet. I ask because, during a time when they didn't ask to be victims or subject to national or media attention, their very real financial needs or family dysfunctions come hand in hand with the blow of racism. Why do I know? Because I came from the same kind of family, and while I've been lucky not to have a family member killed, I know what it's like for family to face prison time. I know a mother's anxiety. I know what it's like to not have health insurance or emergency savings. The problems that the Black community faces on a daily basis is not social policy to them; it's real life. It's the reality show no one wants to watch.

When George Floyd died in police custody, members of the Black community—Tyler Perry, Robert Smith, and others—stepped up to help the family cover the funeral and travel costs. The Black community doesn't have a police union; we are our own union. I call Ben Crump Black America's attorney general because Attorney General William Barr only works for Trump. We need more civil rights attorneys like Crump who do the work because they're in the business of civil rights not settlements. Justice is the only settlement we're interested in.

In the wake of George's death, we've seen a push to defund the police. The word "defund" is a misnomer. What protesters want is a reallocation of budgets and resources to help defang the police. It doesn't mean eliminating the jobs of police officers. It means moving money away from programs that don't work and toward social services that do. It means taking a hard look at the way policing has been managed in this country, and addressing its systemic racism. The GOP will use those three words—defund the police—to drum up old scare tactics. Trump is already spinning it, suggesting that protesters and Democrats are radicals who want to get rid of emergency services. There's nothing radical about expecting the police to serve and protect all Americans and not to brutalize, choke, or kneel on the country's Black citizens. In 2014, 33 percent of Americans believed the police were more likely to use excessive force against Blacks. After George's death, a Monmouth poll shows that number at 57 percent. Out of step with the majority, Trump denied that systemic problems existed, declaring that 99.9 percent of police officers are great people. No one is saying all cops are bad. I'm not even saying most cops are bad. I'm saying there has to be accountability—not just in our neighborhoods but also on the federal level. Police are given a state badge and a state-sanctioned gun, so we have the right to expect that they aren't going to be ruled by impulsive, reckless, or racist behavior. Otherwise, they shouldn't be given state privileges that citizens don't have. So, let's not play that game. And to question them is to make you the enemy? I say to not question them makes you the enemy.

At the level of federal legislation, I stand by the bill introduced by Democratic lawmakers aimed at ending excessive use of force and misconduct by police officers across the country. It is the most expansive intervention into policing I've seen in my lifetime, and includes proposals I've personally been championing for decades: restrictions to prevent police officers from using deadly force except as a last resort, curbing legal protections that shield officers who've been accused of misconduct from being prosecuted, starting a federal registry of police misconduct that requires states to report use of force to the US Justice Department, banning the use of choke holds and carotid holds, among other provisions, including classifying lynching as a federal hate crime. I would also like to see the creation of an empowered, civilian complaint-review board that has the power to hire and fire as well as the creation of a division separate from the locally elected offices to handle any case with a criminal investigation. I think it should be a requirement for police to live in the county they serve. I want this kind of legislation put in place more than anything else because the day I don't have to deliver another eulogy for the Stephon Clarks and the George Floyds of the world is the day I know can die myself.

Voter Suppression

Many of today's Republicans have deliberately engaged in and supported voter suppression campaigns both large and small—changing voting hours, introducing unwieldy identification requirements, curbing the rights for those on probation or parole, gerrymandering—to make voting more difficult for minorities, especially Blacks who, despite being the target of voter suppression, still have decent turnout rates. In 2013, the Supreme Court dismantled key federal protections, including portions of the Voting Rights Act, making it easier than ever for state lawmakers to enact laws about how and when you can vote in a federal election. Some states and localities have a long history of discrimination when it comes to changing voting procedures that leave minorities without a voice at the ballot box. Texas, Georgia, and Ohio are but three states seeking to capitalize on the Trump administration's voter suppression tactics by purging thousands of voters from the rolls. In fact, on the day that George Floyd's family buried him, thousands of votes were being buried in Georgia's primary election, with some voters standing in line for hours only to be faced with malfunctioning voting machines or worse. It was a catastrophe and, with Black-majority neighborhoods experiencing some of the worst problems, nothing short of disenfranchisement. It's a different kind of choke hold but it's a choke hold nonetheless. To distract the American people away from these acts of suppression, Republicans often talk of voter fraud. According to repeated nonpartisan research, voter fraud is nonexistent. In the US, your voice is your vote. The only frauds here are those politicians who betray the ideals of the American experiment to disavow the voice of its people.

REPARATIONS

In April 2019, I invited a dozen of the Democratic presidential nominees to the National Action Network convention to speak to a variety of issues like criminal-justice reform, health care, and the bill HR 40, the Commission to Study Reparation Proposals for African Americans Act, which was first introduced by Congressman John Conyers in 1989. Conyers intentionally chose the number 40 for this bill because it represented the forty acres and a mule that the government had initially promised freed slaves. Not only did this promise go unfulfilled but there has also never been a formal reckoning of the devastation slavery wreaked on the lives of generations of Black families in this country. Every Democratic candidate said they would support the bill. The reason I want to see HR 40 pass is that it acknowledges the fundamental moral injustice and inhumanity of slavery in the United States and allows us to fully examine its repercussions on the Black community. We can debate what reparations would look like, their validity, and how we could implement them today. What we haven't done is formally acknowledge the immorality of slavery nor the profound debt owed to the Black men and women who helped build America with their blood, sweat, tears, and unpaid labor. The fact is over four million Africans and their descendants were enslaved in the colonies from 1619 to 1865, and because of their labor, the United States quickly became one of the most prosperous countries in the world.

Ten years ago, the idea of reparations wasn't a serious part of the national discourse, certainly not on the main stage of a debate among presidential hopefuls. Ten years ago, as a presidential hopeful myself, I was visiting Liberia and Ghana with an entourage that included the scholar Cornel West, Archbishop King, Reverend Al Sampson, and the conservative FOX host Tucker Carlson, among others. Back then, Carlson was a journalist and had been sent to cover my peacekeeping efforts in Liberia's brutal civil war. My mission, unfortunately, had been largely thwarted before our plane even touched the tarmac: Charles Taylor lost control of the country, and two rebel armies—Liberians United for Reconciliation (LURD) and the Movement for Democracy in Liberia (MODEL)— were breathing down his neck. (Taylor was later sentenced to fifty years in prison by the Special Court of The Hague for crimes including terror, murder, and rape.) Days of intense negotiations fell to the wayside after the rebels wouldn't agree to a cease-fire. It was an intense trip that ended with us paying homage to our ancestors at the slavery museum at Cape Coast Castle, the former British customhouse that served as a holding pen for slaves bound for the Americas.

I've often thought back to the moment when I walked down the stone steps of that slaves' dungeon. It was like being inside a cave, dark and hot, with a lone window some fifteen feet or more up the wall that might as well not have been there. At the time I didn't think it was strange to stand in a circle at one of slavery's most infamous sites, singing "We Shall Overcome" with Tucker Carlson, the self-described "whitest man in America." (For the record: I'm not sure Carlson sang with us but, to his credit, he didn't back out of the circle when, one by one, my colleagues and I broke down in tears.) Carlson was simply along for the ride, trying to drum up good copy and eager to see what kind of adventures awaited Al Sharpton in war-torn Africa. For my colleagues and me, however, the slave dungeon wasn't a tourist site. Our crying and singing weren't for the benefit of the whitest man in America or to give him good copy. Though he would later write about us as caricatures and our exploits as satire, that's not how we saw ourselves or the situation. We were human beings reconciling the gravity of slavery. For us, it was real. As the place of no return, that dungeon represented the beginning and the end for so many of our ancestors. We spoke openly to Carlson on that trip, each of us in our own way, confronting the legacy of slavery and the politics of the time with the one white man in our midst. I tell this story to friends and colleagues as a way of saying we are more entwined than we think, know, or profess to know. I was not born a slave, but my ancestors were. Carlson himself wasn't born a slave master, and I don't claim to know anything about his ancestors. The average, modern-day white person may not be guilty of the original crime of slavery, but he or she has enjoyed the advantages that come from decades of not being treated like a Black man or woman in America.

Whenever I speak to white folk about the idea of reparations, I hear a common complaint: "But I wasn't alive in 1700. How can I be blamed for something I didn't do?" The modern white family may not have caused the slavery of the 1700s, but they've benefited from it whether they know it or not. Think of it this way: you yourself may not have robbed a bank, but the money you used to buy the house you're living in came from a bank robbery. It was passed down to you. And let's not forget that when white folk first arrived in America, they were given land: the headright system of 1618, for example, wooed Europeans to Virginia in exchange for land. The Homestead Act of 1862, which provided land in the West, disproportionately favored whites. Like-minded policies and programs, designed by and for whites, gave this community a leg up when America was first coming together. The least we can do as a country is acknowledge the advantages that came with slavery for those who were in power and address the disadvantages among the powerless. Let's say another thief tries to rob a bank but gets caught. Before the lawyers negotiate the criminal sentence or possible restitution, they first address the nature of the crime itself. In a similar fashion, let's acknowledge that slavery was a crime. So long as we keep denying that simple fact, there's no way we can have a real conversation about what is owed to whom.

Back in Washington, DC, Carlson brought his daughter to hear me preach. I've often been amazed that the same group of conservatives who lambaste me on television can nonetheless turn the other cheek outside the studio.

4

CATALYSTS FOR CHANGE:

Women's Rights, #MeToo, and Toxic Masculinity

On March 5, 2020, Elizabeth Warren, the last serious female contender for the Democratic nominee for president, suspended her campaign. A senator and former law professor, she built her campaign on fighting corruption and taking on our country's vast economic inequities. Her progressive vision was, like Bernie Sanders's campaign, sweeping in its scope. Her campaign slogan—Dream Big, Fight Hard—captured her plan for large-scale change. And, as we've seen in the wake of the COVID-19 pandemic, many of her ideas no longer seem as revolutionary as they are necessary. In New York, the people who have suffered the most from COVID-19 are those in low-income areas where residents live as large, multigenerational families in small apartments, making self-isolation and social distancing nearly impossible. Most low-income workers don't have health insurance and are largely still out on the job, making food deliveries, bagging groceries, or packing products at shipping warehouses. These hourly-wage workers are at the frontline of a pandemic where two-thirds of the rest of America can comfortably work from home. The Trump administration decided not to reopen the Affordable Care Act's Healthcare.gov marketplaces, a move that would have made it easier for people who recently lost their jobs to obtain health insurance during a special enrollment period. And while Congress passed the Coronavirus Aid, Relief, and Economic Security Act (CARES), a $2 trillion stimulus package, Trump fired Glenn Fine from his role as the acting inspector general appointed to oversee spending, making it likely that, with little oversight, the taxpayer money will be shelled out to big corporations and political allies. The LA Lakers and Shake Shack, for example, received millions of dollars whereas local Black- and Latino-owned businesses have gotten next to nothing. Following criticism that smaller restaurants were being overlooked by the federal government, Shake Shack did the honorable thing and returned its $10 million small business loan. The Trump administration deflected the federal government's role in managing the crisis and pitted states against one another to source and purchase lifesaving medical equipment. Now, more than ever before, we need more oversight and less corruption in our federal government. Whether you agree with Medicare for All or not, we need a comprehensive health plan that works for everyone. And we need to address the systemic economic disparities in our country. Not tomorrow, not in two weeks. Now. Liz understands this.

I first spoke with Liz at length in Montgomery, Alabama, in 2013. I'd seen her and spoken with her prior to then, but mainly just in passing. Each year, Representative John Lewis brings a delegation of people from Washington, DC, to re-create the historic march of 1965, when protesters and Alabama state troopers clashed on the Edmund Pettus Bridge. As I stood in the lobby of my hotel on the morning of that year's memorial march, I heard my name being called. When I turned, Liz was waving me over to say hello. Her manner was collegial and warm. At the time, there was some rumbling that perhaps she would join the race for president. Hillary would, of course, grab that torch and run with it, but I could tell even then that Liz was seriously contemplating the endeavor. Later that same day, I saw her on the bridge linked arm in arm with my fellow civil rights leaders.

When she dropped out of the race for the Democratic nomination in 2020, a reporter asked her to speak to the role that gender played in the race. She answered, "Gender in this race, you know, is the trap question for any woman. If you say, 'Yeah, there was sexism in this race,' everyone says, 'Whiner!' And if you say, 'No, there was no sexism,' about a bazillion women think, *What planet do you live on?*" The only solution for us to get rid of that trap question is to elect a woman as president. When we speak about *electability*, what we're really talking about is our sexism. A woman is electable if we elect her. Simple as that. Her name is up in the air as the person Democrats would most like to see on the 2020 ticket as vice president. Liz isn't the only one in the running, however. In March 2019 I attended the Selma commemoration at the historic Brown Chapel AME Church, which was Martin Luther King Jr.'s headquarter church in 1965. There were several speakers that day, including Joe Biden, Stacey Abrams, and myself. In my opening remarks, I first gave my respects to the pastor of the church and then to the vice president. I quipped, "I'm not talking about you, Joe. I'm talking about Stacey."

As someone who's spent a lifetime giving speeches, I recognize Stacey's quick-thinking skills as an orator. Besides being eloquent, she's also approachable. People are genuinely drawn to her. I witnessed this firsthand during trips to Georgia where folks of all races in tiny towns like Augusta, Toccoa, and Watkinsville told me they voted for her. I believe she could have won the gubernatorial election in Georgia had the election not been clouded by allegations of voter suppression. We've never had a Black woman on the ticket though there are several qualified contenders besides Stacey, like Kamala Harris and Val Demings. Biden's VP pick is significant; he'll likely be a one-term president, and the next in line had better be able to go the distance with a strong finishing kick.

There are some who believe that Liz suffered from the backlash of Hillary's loss—that people were shy to support a woman again, especially in a race against Trump, a man who weaponizes sexism for political gain. People feared he'd play off the gender card and make Liz an easy target. "Pocahontas" and all that. That may be so, but as long as I've been alive, I've seen the same tropes rolled out whenever a woman steps forward. It doesn't matter if she's progressive, moderate, Republican, white, Black, mixed, gay, straight, religious, or atheist. What we forget is that Trump's election sparked a worldwide protest the day after he was inaugurated. Over seven million people rose up around the world to stand with women: the Women's March, a global referendum on women's rights and human rights, was one of the largest single-day protests in US history, and was followed in short order by a wave of change, including the #MeToo movement and the ouster of several titans of industry for allegations of sexual abuse, harassment, and assault. The gender-equality movement that erupted after Trump was elected was a statement against Trump himself—a man who boasted of grabbing women's private parts and aligned himself with conservative groups to limit women's right to choose—but it was also bigger than him. It was a movement built upon generations of other moments and marches in history when women and men rose up to demand justice for women. A record number of women were elected to Congress in the 2018 midterm elections, flipping seats and taking names across the country. The political rise of Stacey Abrams in Georgia, Alexandria Ocasio-Cortez in New York, along with other new members, like Ilhan Omar of Minnesota, Ayanna Pressley of Massachusetts, and Rashida Tlaib of Michigan wasn't incidental. It was real change, hard fought. Women are ready to lead. It's not women who aren't ready to be elected; we're the problem. We're the electorate forestalling their progress and, by extension, our own.

HAVE FAITH

On Election Night 2016, Aisha and I decided to watch the returns with Hillary Clinton's camp at New York's Javits Convention Center. We knew the evening promised to be historic and wanted to be there when Hillary was elected the first female president of the United States. The Javits Center was teeming with activity when we arrived. There was a palpable sense of excitement. Everyone was gathered to see the breaking of the "highest, hardest glass ceiling," as Clinton referred to a woman someday winning the presidency. The convention center is an all-glass building, and I'd heard that Clinton's team planned to release iridescent shard–like confetti from air canons when she won. Little girls paraded around the convention center, dressed in their Sunday best. Women and men of all stripes were huddled together, talking excitedly. There was already a feeling of victory in the air. Earlier that day, groups of voters had made a pilgrimage to Susan B. Anthony's gravesite in Rochester, New York, to honor the activist who had fought for women's suffrage, leaving behind bouquets of flowers and *I Voted* stickers. The tributes to Anthony had begun earlier that summer when Hillary accepted the Democratic presidential nomination—the first time in history a woman had won the nomination from a major political party.

Aisha and I made our way to the banquet area and saw people standing in a long line, waiting for food. As I pondered how we were going to navigate our way through the throngs of people, my girlfriend gently reminded me that we had been invited to a smaller, more intimate private party at Cipriani Downtown. While I understood the significance of watching Hillary break the proverbial glass ceiling under the literal glass ceiling of the Javits Center, I also longed for a little quiet and a place where I could observe what was going on. We headed downtown. When we left Javits, Hillary had won Delaware, Maryland, New Jersey, Massachusetts, and Rhode Island.

The party at Cipriani Downtown was hosted by Robert De Niro, Jay Penske, and Harvey Weinstein. Rihanna stopped by. Penske, the owner of Penske Media Corporation (PMC) had rented the entire restaurant for about fifty guests, including Paul McCartney, Martha Stewart, and other celebrities, industry titans, and public figures. At the time, of course, the movie mogul Weinstein was a prominent donor to Hillary's campaign and to the Democrat Party and had yet to be brought up on sexual assault charges.

I had barely settled in when Naomi Campbell turned to me and asked, "Al, is she going to lose?" I looked at the television screen. By the time we had left Javits and arrived at Cipriani's, Trump had started to win key states. Ohio was called in Trump's favor. When Florida went to Trump, the guests booed. The mood in the room shifted as the clock inched closer to midnight. I couldn't bear to watch. All I could think was *We elected this guy?* A man who called sexual abuse the stuff of locker-room talk. A man who regularly insulted women on the basis of their gender and looks. *This* was the guy who was going to forestall Hillary breaking the glass ceiling? My only solace was the fact that I wasn't subject to the glare of lights and cameras at the Javits Center and could instead nurse my disbelief in a darkened, semiprivate room. As the numbers began to turn, models and celebrities began making panicked calls to their personal stylists and publicists, canceling their Inauguration Day wardrobes and plans. After a while, Aisha and I called it a night. We didn't speak on the ride home. I think we were simultaneously shell-shocked and in a state of denial. As a reverend, I'm not above believing in miracles and hoped one might still be delivered by the time I woke the following morning.

In every way, Hillary's run was unprecedented, historic on a grand scale. Her concession speech was no different: in the sixty-four-year history of televised presidential concession speeches, she was the only candidate to say *I'm sorry*. Was it a coincidence that the only candidate to apologize for their loss was also a woman? I don't know, but her words—"This is not the outcome we wanted or we worked so hard for, and I'm sorry that we did not win this election for the values we share and the vision we hold for our country"—acknowledged a general failure to beat back the threat of Trump's nativism, misogyny, and general disregard for the Constitution and American democracy. Wrapped up in her apology was a collective feeling of grief and sadness—not for her campaign or herself per se but for the country at large. Think about it: when Trump was afforded the opportunity to apologize for birtherism at a 2016 campaign debate in Hempstead, New York, he refused and congratulated himself instead, saying,

"I was the one that got him to produce the birth certificate, and I think I did a good job."

Toward the end of her speech, Hillary quoted the Bible, Galatians 6:9: "Let us not grow weary in doing good, for in due season, we shall reap if we do not lose heart." She asked us to have faith in one another to continue the fight—not just every four years but every day—to build, in her words, an America that's "hopeful, inclusive, and big-hearted." She called on the young women and girls who were watching, saying that the glass ceiling would one day be shattered, and perhaps sooner than we thought. She told them that they were valuable and powerful and deserving of every chance and opportunity in the world. Her message was gracious in its defeat. At a time when she could have been selfish in her pain, she called upon our greater good because, in her words, "fighting for what's right is worth it." When Hillary ran in 2008 and lost the Democratic Party nomination to Barack Obama, she said that the glass ceiling had eighteen million cracks in it, the same number of votes she'd received. Winning the popular vote in 2016 by about three million votes, you could say the ceiling got hit a few more times. How many more does it need to come down?

In my opinion, history was robbed of witnessing the election of the first female president. I thought of how many other times in history women had been close to making a breakthrough but hadn't. Besides Hillary, there was Victoria Woodhull, the first woman to run, in 1872; Margaret Chase Smith, a Republican, who was the first female candidate for a major party's nomination, in 1964; Charlene Mitchell, the first Black woman to run, in 1968, followed by Shirley Chisholm, who, in 1972, became the first Black candidate for a major party's nomination; and Lenora Fulani, who became the first woman and the first Black candidate to achieve ballot access in all fifty states. And then, of course, there's the record-breaking group of 2020 Democratic nominees: Senator Elizabeth Warren of Massachusetts; Senator Kamala Harris of California; Senator Amy Klobuchar of Minnesota; Senator Kirsten Gillibrand of New York; Representative Tulsi Gabbard of Hawaii; and author Marianne Williamson. I have spoken to and know most of these women. I've known Hillary for years. Liz and I speak regularly. Kamala and I go way back and hit it off immediately—not only does she have top-tier credentials but she's also warm and charismatic. We were introduced to each other by Paula Walker Madison, an NBC News executive near and dear to me who helped NAN honor Kamala when she was running for attorney general in California. Over the years, Kamala and I have had several conversations on race, gender, the criminal-justice system—you name it. Even though she's a prosecutor, she seems genuinely committed to reforming the criminal-justice system, perhaps because she's witnessed some of its flaws and biases firsthand. Of all these politicians, however, Shirley Chisholm has influenced me the most. I learned more about politics from Mrs. C. than from any man, and I know I'm not the only man who can say that. She schooled us.

UNBOUGHT AND UNBOSSED

When I was a teenager, Bishop Washington encouraged me to work with the Congress of Racial Equality (CORE), and it was through that organization that I first met Mrs. C. I called her Mrs. C. from the start. She called me Alfred, which always made me feel both younger and older than my fourteen years. She took a liking to me almost immediately. "The boy preacher!" she'd say. A former teacher, her manner was disciplined and firm, yet caring. She was forever telling me to sit up straight and to clean up my grammar. I always stood a little taller when Mrs. C. was around. "Words matter, Alfred," she'd say. "Use them correctly." Her life as an educator paved her way into politics, where she initially volunteered for several organizations like the Bedford-Stuyvesant Political League and the League of Women Voters, before moving on to become a member of the New York State Assembly.

In 1968, she ran for the House of Representatives from New York's Twelfth Congressional District. The district had recently been redrawn by court mandate; the area had previously been split four ways into districts that diluted the Black vote. To help get a Black leader in office, a citizens' committee was formed whose primary concern was to prevent electing the kind of "Tom" that might appease the larger Kings Country political machine but who wouldn't satisfy the needs of the Black and brown residents themselves. The committee endorsed Mrs. C., viewing her as someone who couldn't be bought by the political establishment. She wasn't afraid of a little controversy or confrontation if it meant doing the right thing. In other words, she was a tree-shaker.

After defeating two Black opponents, State Senator William S. Thompson and labor official Dollie Robertson, Mrs. C. faced Republican James Farmer in the general election. A veteran of the 1960s Freedom Rides in the South and a leading activist in the civil rights movement, Farmer was also the former national chairman of CORE and a well-known national figure. His campaign was a well-oiled machine and wealthy. He, however, had never lived in Brooklyn, and that made a difference. For the campaign, he rented a Brooklyn apartment for the sake of appearances, but the people knew where he lay his head, and it wasn't in Bed-Stuy. Bishop Washington had me work with Farmer because of their shared background with CORE. For whatever reason, I caught the eye of Mrs.

C. during that time, and would later have the good fortune to work with her as her youth director. Farmer hired trucks that drove around the neighborhood streets blaring his campaign message from loudspeakers while Mrs. C. and her volunteers walked the streets of Williamsburg, Crown Heights, and Bedford-Stuyvesant, talking to people and telling them her story. Liz Warren ran her campaign in a similar style, taking the time for selfies and speaking with people one-on-one. Mrs. C.'s campaign slogan, which would later become the title of her autobiography, was Unbought and Unbossed and told voters everything they needed to know about her. Farmer wouldn't know what hit him.

While Farmer collected big bucks from big donors, Mrs. C. collected funds from the local bingo groups, collectives of domestic workers, the PTAs, just average people getting by. Eighty percent of the registered voters in the Twelfth District, which included her own neighborhood of Bedford-Stuyvesant, were Democrat. That edge certainly helped her, not to mention the fact that for every man registered in the district, there were 2.5 women. Mrs. C. also spoke Spanish fluently, which gave her a direct line to the Puerto Rican and Latino communities. She was the embodiment of one of the most important tenets of activism: she was part of the community she wanted to change. She had skin in the game. She spoke to the people in her district. She listened, and then, when she had a megaphone of her own, she spoke up for them. Another big lesson I learned from her was the importance of having Black leadership represent the Black community. This is true even today: while we need more Black CEOs, Black leadership isn't dependent on those Black Americans who can make it in the white-dominated corporate world. Corporate leadership is one thing—and any Black CEO is beholden to the corporate interest he or she serves. Black leadership, however, depends on those individuals who are working to advance the social, economic, and political well-being of the Black community, not any one corporation.

We need more women and more Black leaders in office and the corporate world, but we also need more people on the outside of those institutions willing to help beat down the doors. The only reason we've gotten as far as we have is because someone else paid the fare. Obama's advancement sprang from John Lewis walking across the bridge in Selma. Shirley Chisholm helped pave the way for Kamala Harris. There wouldn't be Blacks in high offices had it not been for Blacks on the streets, who consolidated their voices and showed up to vote. There wouldn't be Blacks in the corporate world if we hadn't organized boycotts against stores that had discriminatory hiring practices. There wouldn't be women in political office if there hadn't been waves of activists pushing for the vote. The fewer people we have organizing on the outside of the corporate and political worlds, the fewer we also have on the inside, working their way up the corporate ladders and navigating the political hierarchy. Mrs. C. was an insider and an outsider both; she was an insider among her constituents, the Black community, and an outsider to the majority-white male Congress. How she walked that tightrope I'll never know. As President Obama said when he posthumously awarded her the Presidential Medal of Freedom, "There are people in our country's history who don't look left or right, they just look straight ahead."

Mrs. C. won with a two-to-one margin over Farmer. Addressing her supporters and volunteers after her victory, she said, "As a result of the sacrifices you have made, as a result of the encouragement you have given me constantly, and as a result of the sores on your feet as you trekked the streets of this community, that you will never regret having worked to send your humble servant, Shirley Chisholm, to fight for you on the national level. Because I recognize how I came and from whence I came, and all I want to do is have you vindicate the faith and the trust that you have placed in me." She was the first Black women to go to Congress and the only woman in the freshman class that year. Even if she'd never opened her mouth again, that fact alone made her headline material. Thank God Mrs. C. didn't have the heart for staying silent.

In 1972, Mrs. C. made her run for president, and I worked as one of her campaign youth coordinators, meeting prominent feminist leaders of the time like Bella Abzug, Fannie Lou Hamer, and Julia Belafonte. I will never forget being a young boy standing on a street median in Manhattan with Mrs. C. and Gloria Steinem and looking up to see one of Bella Abzug's magnificent hats crowding out the sun as we made our way to a protest.

Mrs. C. was a leader, a catalyst for change. Full stop. And, yet, she had trouble mustering the support of what should have been her most obvious backers—women and Blacks—when she ran for president: I saw her grapple with sexism firsthand in meetings with older Black male civil rights leaders and clergymen. In her book *The Good Fight*, she wrote about how Black male leaders had a zero-sum interpretation of Black women's politics and wanted to know one thing only: Would she be a candidate for Blacks or for women? Her colleagues in the Congressional Black Caucus didn't back her, nor did the NAACP, citing her *electability*: they thought she wouldn't be able to beat Nixon. When Jesse Jackson ran for president in 1988, the civil rights establishment didn't support him either, and when I mounted my campaign in 2004, Jesse didn't support me. People who take the next step forward usually have to do it on their own, but sometimes the obstacles in place are far larger than any one thing an individual represents. With Mrs. C., she not only had to wrestle with sexism in the Black community, but also with racism from white female voters. It's a predicament Kamala Harris is familiar with. She and I spoke at length during her run for the Democratic nomination, and much of what she said could have come out of Mrs. C.'s mouth fifty years ago. Besides sexism and racism, the issue of Mrs. C.'s electability kept raising its ugly head: a female voter speaking to the *Toledo Sun* in 1972 said, "I want to vote for her. I'm just not sure she'll win against Nixon." That very sentiment could be applied to Liz Warren and Trump today. And while individual members of the National Organization for Women like Gloria Steinem endorsed Mrs. C., the group's official endorsement went to George McGovern. Of the two battles, Mrs. C. often said she felt the brunt of sexism the most. She's said, "This 'woman thing' is so deep. I've found it out in this campaign if I never knew it before."

This two-pronged problem—sexism and racism—isn't easy to detangle. The roots of both were forged together and found a particularly cruel expression in the early days of slavery and the abolitionist movement, with Black women engaging in tribal fighting with their men, who didn't want women to have certain rights that could threaten their sense of manhood or place in the Black family structure. Throughout history, many a Black man has argued that any gain made by the feminist movement for Black women erodes and emasculates Black manhood. Black men have often argued, and some still do, that Black women have to be less than a Black man in order for both to be equal in white America. Sadly, this worldview is often supported by the Black church. Reverend Wyatt Tee Walker was one of the few Baptist ministers who freely welcomed women into the pulpit. Bishop Washington was also an exception and invited women into the church as preachers. In the course of my life, I've watched the Black church slowly evolve on the issues, but at great personal pain to its congregants. Historically speaking, the Black church has been deeply exclusionary toward the advancement of its women, a sentiment that was echoed by some of the early civil rights leaders. Women weren't invited to the March on Washington in 1963, and they had just as much at stake as the Black men.

On the other side, the earliest days of the suffragist movement weren't welcoming to Black women either, with white women largely wanting to be equal to their men while still being able to enjoy the gains granted to them by racism and the forced labor of Black women. As groups, Blacks and women were both fighting for the right to vote at the same time in history, and their uneasy jockeying often pitted one against the other, with Susan B. Anthony famously stating, "I will cut off this right arm of mine before I will ever work or demand the ballot for the Negro and not the woman." History isn't clean: this is the same woman whose tombstone was covered with celebratory *I Voted* stickers for Hillary's 2016 presidential run. A victory for some is never a victory for all or, as Sojourner Truth said, "I feel that I have the right to have just as much as a man. There is a great stir about colored men getting their rights, but not a word about colored women; and if colored men get their rights, and colored women not theirs, the colored men will be masters over the women, and it will be just as bad as it was before." So, yes, there have been contradictions in the women's movement based on race, and yes, there have been contradictions in the civil rights movement based on misogyny, but it's better to be engaged in the tension between the two movements to see where and how each side can come to the table and either hash out their differences or put them aside to make room to fight in the name of liberation for all. Think of it this way: you and I have lunch together and decide to walk to Forty-Second Street and Seventh Avenue. We're in agreement on our final destination. We can debate all the way to Forty-Second Street whether or not I should put on my coat and gloves or if you should remove your hat. We can even argue about which route to take. But what we can't argue about is the destination itself. If you decide, no, I think I'll head to Bryant Park instead, we're divided, and no end will come from us saying we want the same thing but then work against ourselves to get there. Once there's even a sliver of an opening in our stance—once we are no longer a people united—there's space for someone like Donald J. Trump to pit us against one another until we're no longer sure where we were headed in the first place. We end up crosstown staring at one another, waving our hats and gloves and coats in the air.

In many respects, Mrs. C. was the forerunner of modern Black feminism. If it hadn't been for Shirley, there couldn't have been a Kamala Harris or a Stacey Abrams. There may not even have been a President Obama. She took the hits that normalized the idea that Blacks could perform at high-level jobs and have political careers, and she did it without compromise. Her strength as a trailblazer came from a sense of deep personal pride and self-awareness, which paralleled the cultural message of feminism in the 1960s and 1970s. A petite woman, she nonetheless possessed a formidable presence. When she walked into a room, she made an entrance like she knew she was breaking a barrier just by being there. She was fond of saying, "If they don't give you a seat at the table, bring a folding chair." You got the sense that she'd carried around a lot of folding chairs in her life and was used to people being shocked when she took her seat. In this sense, she and Hillary Clinton remind me of each other. In personal encounters, they share a quiet dignity that manifests itself in physical form: their bearing is erect yet reserved. They both know their very presence—in a boardroom, on a national stage, in a classroom—will engender some kind of reaction, good or bad, from women and from men, and they brace themselves for it. The truth is, Hillary walks into a room and sizes everyone else up. In their discomfort, she's supremely comfortable, and that takes confidence and finesse. She projects a facade of stillness that can be misinterpreted for rigidity when in truth she's the embodiment of the Latin proverb *Still waters run deep.* There's a depth to her—in thought, in principle, and in the strength of her convictions; I saw this up close when she came out swinging for health care when Bill was in office. She and Mrs. C. share that sense of passion and sentient self-assurance. They're both dignified yet firm. Brave.

In an interview given before her death in 2005 at the age of eighty, Mrs. C. spoke about how she wanted to be remembered, saying, "I want history to remember me not just as the first Black woman to be elected to Congress, not as the first Black woman to have made a bid for the presidency of the United States, but as a Black women who lived in the twentieth century and dared to be herself. I want to be remembered as a catalyst for change in America." We should all be so courageous to be unbought and unbossed to the very end.

Words Become Deeds

Shirley Chisholm wasn't the only woman to have a lasting effect on me, nor was she the last to admonish me for my grammar. In 1999, I had a series of long and meaningful conversations with Coretta Scott King. She spoke with me at the urging of her son, Martin Luther King III, who had fought many civil rights battles with me. Long after her husband had been killed, Coretta visited me in New York City to talk about my civil rights work and my plans to advance the National Action Network. We spoke generally for some time, and then she settled back into her chair and leveled her gaze at me. In her quiet and gentle yet firm and regal voice, she asked me about some of my past controversies. She questioned me in a way that I knew was sincere. She was genuinely invested in trying to understand where I was coming from, and in her simple and direct manner, she reminded me of Mrs. C. Here I was, a grown man feeling like a teenager again, trying to explain why I'd done and said some of the things I had. She went down the list, turning over every stone, asking me to clarify details. I kept having to contextualize some of my past language to her. I told her I didn't mean anything by it; it was just the way we spoke on the streets.

After she listened to my explanations, she finally said, "Al, don't you realize words have power?" I defended myself and said that I was just speaking in the rhythm and the style of the time. She wasn't having it. She said, "You've got to learn to filter what you say for the long-term gain and not sell it for the short-term satisfaction of being theatrical or for getting attention. Otherwise, you could win the crowd but lose the crown." She explained herself further, saying, "If you and the people you're fighting have the same kind of language, calling each other bigoted, derogatory names, then what's the difference?"

Not everyone gets lectured by Coretta Scott King, and so I took the lesson seriously. I dedicated myself to the task of dropping my inflammatory language and, with it, some of my attitude. This isn't to say I dropped the fight; on the contrary, it made me more focused and determined. But listen: some of my closest friends are rappers and singers. I grew up around James Brown. It was hard for me to break my habit. Worse, many of my friends challenged my position, saying that it was free speech to use the B-word, the N-word in their songs. "Look at it this way," I'd explain. "Do the record execs let you use that language on them? Then, why is it okay for us to denigrate our own community, our sisters? We're doing the work for them."

Over the years, I became close with the King family. When Corettta turned seventy, the family invited me to attend her birthday dinner at Paschal's in Atlanta. I was honored to have been seated next to her. I'm sure the seating arrangements were set up by Martin Luther King III. At dinner, she leaned in close and asked quietly, "How are we doing with our language, Al?"

"We're doing better," I said.

She smiled and patted my hand. "Better ain't there yet, but I'll take it for tonight."

Several years later, Coretta asked if I could help her daughter, Yolanda, who was an actress, book a show at the Apollo. Because of James Brown, I've had a long-standing relationship with the theater and arranged it to host a NAN convention with Yolanda as the opening act of the evening. To see Coretta Scott King sitting in the box seats watching her daughter's one-woman play made the evening. Coretta died a few years later, and Yolanda passed away two years after her mother. In his opening remarks for the eulogy for Coretta, Reverend Joseph Lowery said, "I'm not a gambler nor a bettor, but who could have brought this crowd together but Coretta? How marvelous that presidents and governors come to mourn and praise, but in the morning, where words become deeds that meet needs." I couldn't have said it better myself.

DOUBLE DEALING

For me, Barack Obama's 2008 inauguration fulfilled a childhood fascination and dream that a Black man, someone like me, could become president. I had long looked up to men like Adam Clayton Powell Jr. and Jesse Jackson. Mrs. C. looked up to Powell, too, during his heyday. We often indulged in conversations about the cigar-chomping congressman. In these Black men, I saw Obama and vice versa. It felt as if we had finally arrived...after so many years of hard work. A Black president. The way I saw it, Hillary was going to be the fulfillment of Shirley Chisholm. She was the embodiment of everything we told young women to aspire to be: well-educated, driven, and successful, whether she was working as a state prosecutor, a senator, or secretary of state.

But we were trumped.

Trump parlayed his years of being a larger-than-life television star into the greatest show in political history, and his audience—we, the people—were seduced by the entertainment. In Trump's world, he successfully redirected the audience's attention away from the issues and to the performers. In Trump's world, Hillary was a bit character; he's the main attraction. A natural performer, though not necessarily a good one, he's used his one-man show to fan the flames of this country's deepest fears, and that includes good old-fashioned sexism. Trump spent the better part of his term publicizing the 2016 exit polls like he was promoting a new brand of politics, and he was. That new brand was Trump himself. He'll slap his name on anything: steaks, a phony university, democracy. One stat from an exit poll he particularly loved was that 53 percent of white women voted for him in 2016, as if that percentage somehow inoculated him from the suspicion of misogyny. Exit polls are meant to give a real-time snapshot of an election and aren't always accurate. Later analysis by the nonpartisan Pew Research Center showed that the percentage of white women who voted for Trump was actually 47 percent. Still significant, but not by the larger margin Trump purports. The number of nonwhite women who supported Hillary was a big margin of 82 percent to 16 percent. Is it possible that Republican white women, who overwhelmingly supported Trump, voted with racial bias or that they voted in keeping with their men? It's nearly impossible to tease out. This is what I know: Trump's rhetoric toward women and his openly confrontational style with any so-called nasty women who question his actions are sexist and misogynistic at best. Worse, his administration is backing him up, passing legislation that has real-life consequences for women.

Since Trump has been in office, he's focused on defunding Planned Parenthood and gutting the Title X Family Planning Program, a vital source of family planning and related preventive care for low-income, uninsured, and young people across the country; issued a draft Title IX regulation that attempts to silence sexual assault survivors and limit their educational opportunities; and revoked the Obama-era 2014 Fair Pay and Safe Workplaces Executive Order, dismissing protections, like paycheck transparency, and a ban on forced-arbitration clauses for sexual harassment, sexual assault, or discrimination claims for women workers. Women's rights are eroding state by state, issue by issue, especially when it comes to a woman's right to choose.

Now, listen: I'm a preacher, and so, for me, the issue isn't about whether or not you endorse abortion. The issue is about whether or not women have the right to choose. Inherent to the position that women aren't free to choose what to do with their own bodies is the implication that they aren't equal to men and are, therefore, incapable of making their own decisions. You can't have a real commitment to gender equality while simultaneously telling women that they can't make their own decisions or have a stake in their personal agency. Likewise, you can't have a real commitment to gender equality while simultaneously courting financial relationships with predatory men like Harvey Weinstein or with corporations and companies whose business practices put women at a disadvantage. The double dealing has to end.

#METOO

Tarana Burke, a Black woman, activist, and survivor of sexual harassment, created the Me Too movement more than a decade ago. In 2006, while lying across a mattress on the floor of her one-bedroom apartment and tired of the sexual violence she saw in her community, she wrote the words *me too* on a piece of paper, along with an action plan for sexual assault survivors to help build a movement based on empathy. Since then, the movement has morphed into something bigger and less defined, helping to create an atmosphere of accountability and shining a light on high-profile men accused of sexual abuse, harassment, and assault. Unfortunately, as the movement has gotten larger and more hashtag-mainstream, it's also bypassed the experiences of women of color and today is more of a cultural phenomenon, meaning different things to different people, than a political movement with an organized base and legislative reach.

In her 2019 TED Talk, Burke clarified who she initially created the movement for, saying, "This is a movement about the one-in-four girls and one-in-six boys who are sexually assaulted every year and carry those wounds into adulthood. It's about the 84 percent of trans women who will be sexually assaulted this year. And the indigenous women who are three and a half times more likely to be sexually assaulted than any other group. Or people with disabilities, who are seven times more likely to be sexually abused. It's about the 60 percent of Black girls, like me, who will be experiencing sexual violence before they turn eighteen." Most people have heard Martin Luther King Jr.'s famous paraphrasing of abolitionist minister Theodore Parker's 1853 sermon: "The arc of the moral universe is long, but it bends toward justice." As Burke says, "Someone has to do the bending." You cannot have a society built on moral principles where women, with an unequal access to power, can be made to do things against their will or in violation of their person. Whenever someone has power over another individual, they also assume privilege, and it's this unique combination that makes women so vulnerable to sexual harassment and assault. But as Burke points out, power and privilege don't always have to destroy and take. They can also be used to serve and build.

In some respects, I view the #MeToo movement in a similar vein to that of the Black Lives Matter movement, which was created by three Black organizers—Alicia Garza, Patrisse Cullors, and Opal Tometi—after the acquittal of George Zimmerman for the death of Trayvon Martin in 2013. When we talk about Black Lives Matter, are we talking about the real, on-the-ground activism or are we talking about a hashtag on a T-shirt? It started as a response to the callous disregard of Black lives. As a statement, Black Lives Matter doesn't negate the fact that *all* lives matter. Let's be real here: the reason why Black lives matter and the statement was adopted into a movement is because Black lives aren't considered equal to all other lives, both historically and up to the present day. The point here is: Do Black lives matter? This movement says, yes, they do. After George Floyd's death, the movement has morphed into something bigger than itself. The danger is that it can be manipulated and willfully misinterpreted by the mainstream media or anyone who equates activism with wearing a Black Lives Matter T-shirt.

Black Lives Matter is a member-led organization comprised of different branches of activists that respond to core issues that minimize Black life. For all the differences among the movement's activists, Garza, Cullors, and Tometi have built a sound foundation, however, and have been especially proactive at inviting women and gender-fluid individuals to the table. They've been intentional about getting out of their predisposed silos. Similarly, the #MeToo movement isn't one structure; today, it has several tentacles and many branches, though not enough minorities at its top levels. The media, in not doing their homework, has too often confused the real activism of both groups with catchy bumper sticker slogans, turning Black Lives Matter into a general celebration of Black life and the #MeToo movement into something that resembles girl power. (As the country reached its boiling point with the Floyd protests, it's become more and more difficult for the mainstream media to ignore the urgency of Black Lives Matter as a statement, rallying cry, and movement.) Burke initially named the movement Me Too because it spoke to the solidarity of sexual assault survivors, and while empowerment is always good, the danger in equating the movement to something as vague as "girl power" dilutes its real strength and its ability to foster a broad-based coalition.

Both groups are working to transform the larger culture of their respective movements into something with real legislative change. A hashtag isn't real activism; it's a good way to spread information via social media, yes, but every movement needs direct action built into its core. Their respective founders know this, but do their followers? Otherwise, what's the point? Otherwise, you're selling morality for the price of a T-shirt.

Cathy Hughes:
A Woman's Voice for Black America

Most people don't understand that the drumbeat in Black America is Black radio, and if we're talking about

Black radio, we're talking about Cathy Hughes. Cathy grew up in Omaha, Nebraska, one child among many born to Helen and William Woods. Her father was the first Black man to earn an accounting degree from Creighton University, the same college Cathy herself would later attend yet not complete. She got her start in radio working at KOWH AM, a station owned by Black professionals. She started working at an early age and, after stints at Creighton and KOWH, moved to Washington, DC, where she got a job as general sales manager at Howard University's radio station WHUR FM, increasing the station's revenue from $250,000 to $3 million in her first year. She wanted to create and own a radio station of her own, however. Most people would give up after being denied thirty-two times by banks, but not Cathy. She and her husband eventually found a lender and, in 1980, founded Radio One by buying AM station WOL 1450 in Washington, DC. Determined to be the megaphone for Black America, she was undeterred by her early financial difficulties. While she lost her home trying to keep the station afloat, she never lost her voice—the radio.

Cathy not only wanted to protect the voice and contribution of Black culture but she also sought to amplify it and make it impossible to ignore. She could have worked for a different station but, instead, took the moral stance that Black ownership was of paramount importance. She stood at the crossroads of her life and decided that instead of giving up on her dream, she'd commit herself fully to it. She and her young son moved into the station, and she ran her radio show morning, noon, and night. When the bank threatened to take away her funding unless she aired more music, she doubled down, pioneering a new talk show radio format—twenty-four-hour talk from a Black perspective—that later made WOL the most listened-to talk radio in the nation's capital. She rolled the dice. She could have lost it all, but she didn't. She took people like Dick Gregory and put him on the air. She gave Michael Eric Dyson his own show. She put me on the air.

I first met Cathy in the 1980s. After I ran for president, she bought me out of a contract I was under for another radio station based in Chicago and put me on the air the same week. She did not play around. For the past eighteen years for three hours a day, I've used the megaphone Cathy handed me, broadcasting my show to full effect. I don't believe we could have mobilized the movements surrounding Trayvon Martin's death or the Jena Six, Eric Garner, or Michael Bell without having the reach of my radio show. Because of it, we were able to tap into regional networks and broadcast information, mobilize the masses. Black radio has long been utilized by civil rights activists: Martin Luther King Jr., for example, lived below a Black-owned radio station on Auburn Avenue in Atlanta for some time. Whenever King was preparing a rally or a protest, he'd call up to the station, and the DJ would literally lower the mic from the top window down to his window, and he would broadcast the necessary information. Black radio was and still is, in many ways, a link to the underground of American Black culture. I use it to keep my ear to the ground, speaking to and listening for the issues and topics that most affect Black America. Like the Black church, Black radio is the lifeblood of the Black community. It's one of the few places where the Black community can congregate freely to exchange information, celebrate our music and our culture, and talk among ourselves.

Cathy's station became the voice of Black America—she changed the R&B station to a twenty-four-hour talk radio format with the theme Information Is Power, which she hosted for eleven years. She'd later go on to own seventy radio stations in nine markets. By 1999, Radio One was a force and became a publicly traded company listed under the NASDAQ stock exchange, making Cathy the first Black women to chair a publicly held corporation. In 2017, Radio One's name was changed to Urban One, and today, she owns the television network TV One, the largest Black-owned cable television network in the country, along with several other subsidiaries, and she is a minority owner of Black Entertainment Television network.

In the early days of her station, Cathy herself hosted the morning news show from the station's picture window. People would stand below the window to watch her do the show live, cheering and pumping their fists for her in solidarity. Why? People cheered her on because she was lifting the Black voice to maximum volume. She made it impossible for people not to listen to us. And I know it worked, then and now. In 2009, I attended Barack Obama's first inauguration. Afterwards, the congregation filed into a fleet of buses waiting to transport us to the US Capitol for the official inauguration ceremony. While waiting to board, a Black woman approached me. I didn't recognize her, but she knew who I was. "Reverend," she said, "I want to thank you for standing up for the president. It meant a lot to us." She extended her hand and introduced herself. She was Maya Soetoro-Ng, Obama's sister. I knew then that she was thanking me for my endorsement of Obama. I said, "If I didn't believe him, I wouldn't stand up for him." She went on to tell me that she and her family had long listened to me on the radio. I immediately felt the intimacy of the moment—there's something deeply personal about having your voice be welcomed into anyone's home, let alone the family of the soon-to-be forty-fourth president of the United States. In that moment, I felt validated, my message received by families all around the country and echoed back by our progress, and that was largely made possible by Cathy Hughes.

Maya Angelou once said, "Each time a woman stands up for herself, without knowing it possibly, without claiming it, she stands up for all women." I think the same sentiment can be said for a woman's voice: when one woman makes her voice heard, all of America listens. And when millions of women speak up, as they did with #MeToo and the Women's March, tides change.

BE A KING WHEN KINGDOM COMES

I grew up in a single-parent home, and the majority of the men in my life were the role models I sought out: Bishop Washington, Adam Clayton Powell Jr., James Brown, and Jesse Jackson. In a sense, with my father gone, my mother was my mother and father both. As a child, I didn't witness the toxic masculinity that so many of my friends saw in their fathers. My mother managed the household completely, taking care of everything from putting food on the table and paying the bills to teaching me life lessons. It has never been a question for me that women are strong and capable and smart. I've witnessed their strength and intelligence with my own eyes;

most of us have. I was just as close to Shirley Chisholm as I was to Adam Clayton Powell Jr., so I've seen what women can do when they're in charge. That said, I've known many men, close friends, who have struggled in their relationships with women and with their toxic masculinity. I listen and speak with them in the same manner I do with members of my church, offering advice and guidance. Because of my background, I've often found that men can speak a little more openly with me—my personal reference points are a little different. I can explain that while there's a history of toxic masculinity in the Black community, that doesn't make it right. If you need someone to be beneath you in order to feel good about yourself, you're no better than a white slave owner at the post. In many respects, the idea of male superiority is as dangerous as the idea of racial superiority.

Whenever one group of people requires another group to be controlled, denigrated, or put down in order to feel powerful or to maintain their status, it's a problem, and this isn't limited to sexism within the Black community. The right wing, for example, has weaponized this kind of mindset to distract and distort: if a lower-class white man is struggling to make ends meet in a job market that no longer supports his kind of work, well, at least his whiteness and his maleness still afford him a sense of power. Rather than rising up and addressing the issue of income inequality or asking why job-training programs haven't been implemented, the right wing base can instead swivel its attention to the minorities and the women who threaten the white man's identity politics. Nothing gets solved—the white man is still out of a job—and racism and sexism continue unabated.

There's a burden to carrying around toxic masculinity. It reminds me of a famous civil rights adage: once you free the slave, you also free the slave master. Many men I speak with carry the weight of thinking that they have to live up to an idea of manhood with a capital M. This old-school mentality tells men that they have to be in charge, and the woman has to remain submissive or kept in her place. When you have to prove you're a man, you're setting yourself up for failure. There's no winning that game. The more we can move to a relationship model—in our personal and professional lives, and in culture at large—of being partners and coequals, the lesser the burden of gender bias for both women *and* men. In a more equal relationship, men can let go of this dominating model of masculinity. Once that pressure is relieved, he's free to be more creative, innovative, and caring. He can channel the energy and focus he had on keeping the woman down to focus more on himself and becoming the best person—the best version of himself—he knows is possible not only for himself but also for the women in his life and his family. He can be a king when Kingdom comes.

5

UNARMED TRUTH AND UNCONDITIONAL LOVE:

LGBTQ Rights, Homophobia, and the Black Church

Whenever I host my radio show, the one issue that consistently raises the most passionate discussion among Black listeners is that of gay rights. I mention anything about gender-neutral bathrooms, and the phone board lights up. If I switch it up to talk about Ukraine or Robert Mueller, I might get a few callers, the majority of whom usually want me to go back to talking about the bathrooms. If I utter the words *same-sex marriage*, it's like I'm doing a telethon fundraiser: the phone rings off the hook, and each caller is more opinionated than the last. Some callers make the argument that the Black community already has enough issues to deal with, so why add the struggles of the LGBTQ community to our list? If we agree with that sentiment, then why not also ignore the issues surrounding gender equality or income inequality? Why not overlook antidiscrimination laws altogether? Where does it stop? The LGBTQ community isn't a separate entity divorced from the concerns and history of the Black community. In fact, some of the most revolutionary and forward-thinking leaders of the civil rights movement and Black culture were gay. Where would we be without Bayard Rustin, the man behind the March on Washington, or Mandy Carter? Or the works of Langston Hughes, Audre Lorde, or James Baldwin? The magnificence of Billy Porter? Unless you're prepared to say that gays and lesbians aren't human beings, they should have the same constitutional rights of any other human being.

It's true that the Black community struggles with homophobia and, given the trauma of our past, it's understandable why homosexuality is a hot-button topic: the very idea of manhood was stripped from generations of straight Black men during slavery. The emasculation of Black men during slavery was total and complete: a Black man, by law, couldn't marry his partner. Worse, the Black woman was often sexually preyed upon by the slave master, and because the Black man had no rights, he legally couldn't protect her, seek redress, or ask law enforcement for help. To psychologically survive this emasculation, the Black man sought out affirmation of his manhood with a capital M as discussed in the previous chapter. In this light, Black gay men and lesbians can be seen as an affront to the identity of manhood that straight Black men have been trying to reclaim for years. This is a sad state indeed but, within the context of the abuse suffered during the era of slavery, it's also a complicated truth. What if, in affirming his sense of manhood, the Black man is also forced to deny his sexuality and the sexuality of other Black men? Has he truly achieved manhood then? Is it not liberating to say, "I'm a Black man, and my orientation is other men?" Does that statement make a Black man any less of a man? Or "I'm a

Black woman and my orientation is other women?" Is she less of a woman? If you have to deny your orientation and internalize the tension, stress, and trauma of living in that denial, then aren't you reducing yourself? The unarmed truth is this: manhood isn't dependent on one's sexuality, gay or straight, and self-destruction isn't the answer to societal destruction. The same can be said for women. I say this with some knowledge on the subject as I watched Joy, my openly gay sister, struggle with the burden of homophobia throughout her life.

GET IN LINE OR GET OUT OF THE WAY

While my sister's sexuality was never hidden from us, her family, I know she had difficulty navigating her path in the broader world. For me, not accepting my sister was never an option. As a family, we shared each other's burdens. I remember my mother telling me firmly: "She's your sister." Those three words dissipated any doubt I may have had about my sister's lesbianism; she was my sister first. End of story. My mother also pointed out to me the various singers and musicians in the church choir who were gay as well as the choir director himself—their sexuality was widely acknowledged as an open secret. She helped me see the hypocrisy: these individuals were contributing members of the church, and yet, outside its doors, they were treated as second-class citizens and denied equal protections and rights. My mother invited my sister's girlfriends to our family dinners, which normalized the issue for me. The way I saw it, our family's configuration and my sister's orientation were no big thing. If my sister's lesbianism wasn't an issue at home, why was it an issue in public? I wrestled with this question over the years, especially as I balanced some of the language and teachings of the Bible against what I saw and experienced in the world.

Joy was a brilliant artist. Over the years, I watched as the cumulative pressure of dealing with racism, homophobia, and sexism crushed some of her ambition and dampened her creative spark. Of the three burdens, I'm not sure which was the heaviest for her, though I suspect it's difficult to parse out the pain. Later in life, she learned how to gather up enough inner strength to combat the pressures she felt, but this was something she only learned how to manage after years of struggling. It's a particularly heartbreaking situation when the circumstances of your birth—your very existence—carries with it a social stigma so strong that you have to hide the very thing that gives your life affirmation. How can you truly be free if you have to hide who you are to get the acceptance of those you love? It takes years of personal reconciliation and strength-building to get to the point when you decide that you don't need other people's acceptance, that you first and foremost need self-acceptance. Once you've accepted yourself, everyone else can either get in line or get out of the way. My sister decided to love and stand up for herself, and because of it she's stronger today, and by extension, so am I. Speaking more broadly, as a society, we shouldn't be in the business of tearing people down. We need to help bring people up. While individuals like my sister may struggle to come to terms with who they are, the rest of society is tasked with the challenge of meeting them halfway and in helping to ensure that their rights and protections are equal under the law.

The Black community cannot move forward without coming to terms with our gay brothers and sisters. We cannot heal generations of pain and heartache without seeking the forgiveness of those we've forsaken and without opening ourselves—as difficult as that may be for some—to the struggles of the LGBTQ community. According to the Williams Institute, there are more than one million LGBTQ Blacks currently living in the United States, and these men and women face a disproportionate amount of bias, discrimination, and prejudice despite the monumental gains of the civil rights movement. Where a Black sister may experience racism and sexism, a lesbian or trans Black woman must also contend with homophobia or transphobia, which can rear its head in any number of socioeconomic issues, including economic insecurity, violence and harassment, HIV and health inequity, religious intolerance, and police brutality. The data is grim: a 2012 report found that 32 percent of children being raised by Black same-sex couples live in poverty compared to 13 percent of children raised by heterosexual Black parents and 7 percent of married heterosexual white parents; Black transgender women face the highest level of fatal violence within the LGBTQ community and are less likely to turn to police for help; LGBTQ Blacks experience religious intolerance from their own Black community. The very doors that should be opening to them are, instead, slamming shut. Black LGBTQ people who feel marginalized within their own communities are less likely to come out, and this often has dire health ramifications for the group as a whole: not only are fewer studies and less medical research done on the group but LGBTQ medical resources, support, and funding also lag behind. Thankfully, change is happening, and I've personally witnessed some of the evolution. The Human Rights Campaign, for example, recently appointed Alphonso B. David as its president, making him the first civil rights lawyer and person of color to hold that position in the organization's forty-year history. It's one of the few times I can think of where the establishment LGBTQ leadership has embraced Black leadership. From a wider acceptance of LGBTQ leadership in human rights organizations—and even in the Black civil rights movement where gays and lesbians were once shunned—to the creation of LGBTQ-supported churches to a larger percentage of Blacks now supporting same-sex marriage, there's been a shift in public opinion on gay rights, especially within the last decade. Think of where we were not long ago: in 2008, 70 percent of religious Black voters overwhelmingly voted in favor of California's Proposition 8, essentially sinking the issue of same-sex marriage for the state and sparking racial animus between the white gay community and the Black community. Proposition 8 didn't stop the march of progress, however. Five years later, in 2013, then–attorney general Kamala Harris officiated the state's first same-sex marriage ceremony since the enactment of the proposition, and today 51 percent of Blacks support same-sex marriage, according to a 2019 Pew Research Center poll. This shift is attributed, in part, to a wider acceptance of gays in America in general and to Obama's much-publicized evolution of support on same-sex marriage, which, thanks to his administration, is now legal in the United States. With regards to civil rights, the Obama administration was most successful in the arena of gay rights. The accomplishments stacked up: in 2011, President Obama repealed Don't Ask, Don't Tell, initiated by President Clinton in 1992. During his campaign for presidency, Clinton promised he'd lift the ban against gays in the military. Failing to garner enough support for the policy, however, he passed Don't Ask, Don't Tell—a policy first dreamt up by General Colin Powell—that allowed gay men and women to serve in the military as long as they kept their sexuality a secret. President Obama effectively ended seventeen years of secrecy and silence for gay, lesbian, and bisexual service members and lifted the ban on transgender people serving in the military. In 2009, Obama signed into law a new hate crime act known as the Matthew Shepard Act; in 2014, the administration issued an executive order barring federal contractors from discriminating on the basis of sexual orientation or gender identity; and, in 2015, the Pentagon added sexual orientation to the Military Equal Opportunity policy for the first time, meaning gay servicemen and servicewomen would be protected from discrimination.

The shift in acceptance of gay rights has largely been generational. The next generation of up-and-coming leaders have a more inclusive worldview, especially with regards to the fluidity of gender identities, and this is a strength. Leadership comes in all forms—gay, Black, white, trans, Latino, you name it—and it's a benefit to the youth of today that they can both recognize and mobilize a diversity of people in the name of a common goal or initiative. We need more of this kind of thinking in all areas of activism. I may be a member of the old guard, but I'm looking at the generations nipping at my heels. I'm counting on them to grab ahold of the reins and transform the next iteration of social justice into a human rights movement for every gender, sexual orientation, color, and religion.

Bayard Rustin:
Angelic Troublemaker

Most Americans remember Martin Luther King Jr. for his inspirational "I Have a Dream" speech, delivered from the Lincoln Memorial in 1963 at the March on Washington. Lesser known is the man behind the scenes: Bayard Rustin, a civil rights leader who was not only the primary organizational force behind the march but who also introduced Martin Luther King Jr. to the nonviolent resistance tactics of Mahatma Gandhi. Bayard worked out of the public eye in part because his organizational skills made him a particularly good strategist—someone you want working behind the scenes—and in part because he was an openly gay man during an era when homosexual behavior was considered a criminal act. While Martin Luther King Jr. acknowledged Bayard's homosexuality and still worked closely with him, other civil rights leaders weren't so welcoming. In a newly released audio interview with the *Washington Blade* in the mid-1980s, Bayard says, "At any given point, there was so much pressure on Dr. King about my being gay and particularly because I would not deny it that he set up a committee to explore whether it would be dangerous for me to continue working with him." Bayard would later help King create the Southern Christian Leadership Coalition (SCLC) but would be pushed out by other leaders, who were concerned his homosexuality would publicly damage the group. Bayard kept working for the cause, inspired by his Quaker faith that preaches a deep sense of humility in the face of social service. In the Quaker tradition, the notion of credit isn't important; speaking truth to power is. Every community needed, in Bayard's words, "a group of angelic troublemakers."

In 1953, Bayard was arrested on a morals charge. To be known as gay and to have a criminal record for it meant Bayard was ostracized even among the leaders of the Black community who knew him and applauded his civil rights work. Much of his work wasn't credited to him. Long before President Clinton formally introduced it in the military, Don't Ask, Don't Tell was an informal cultural policy in certain circles. Bayard could help organize the movement and the top leaders knew that he did, but his contributions weren't widely publicized. Case in point: Bayard organized the March on Washington, what was then considered the largest demonstration the country had ever seen, in two months. At the march's end, Bayard took to the microphone himself and read a series of demands to President John F. Kennedy. Chief among them was basic civil rights legislation—decent housing, integrated education, fair employment, the right to voice—and no filibuster.

Bayard was big enough to do the work and not get the credit. He wasn't in the movement for self-aggrandizement. He believed in the fight and was dedicated to advancing justice and equality not only for Blacks, but for gays, Latinos, women, and other minorities. More than most, he understood the power of coalition politics and tried to unite labor with the gay-rights movement, which back then was still underground. He championed various movements uniting together to fight the common enemy of injustice, writing: "You have to join every other movement for the freedom of people. Therefore join the movement as individuals against anti-Semitism, join the movements for the rights of Hispanics, the rights of women, the rights of gays. In other words, I think that each movement has to stand on its own feet because it has a particular agenda, but it can ask other people." He was ahead of his time. No doubt about it: Bayard Rustin was the philosophical intellectual forerunner of what we today call intersectionalism, but because of his homosexuality and, to some degree, because of his so-called left-leaning tendencies, he never got his due. He envisioned a coalition of people working together for civil rights just as everyone started to splinter off into political and racialized silos during the Vietnam War.

Over the years, I'd seen Bayard at several events. With his shock of hair, tall and lanky gait, angular face,

and those thick, black-rimmed glasses, he was difficult to miss. By the early 1970s, I was already known
in New York City for some of my early activist work.
At sixteen years old, I wanted to strike out on my own
but was unsure of how to do so. I was involved in various youth initiatives, like getting the voting age lowered from twenty-one to eighteen, which eventually
happened, and sponsoring job programs for youths.
Clarence Jones, Martin Luther King Jr.'s counsel, and
Freeman Moyler, a projects manager for the *New York
Times*, signed incorporation papers for my youth organization. My lawyer, who incorporated my group, was
also an aspiring politician at the time. His name was
David Dinkins, who would, of course, go on to become
New York's first and, to date, only Black mayor. If it
seems unusual that men three times older than I was
would be in the business of incorporating a teenage
boy's youth-activist group, it was. But, then, I was unusual, too. A reporter once asked Dinkins how he could
take a sixteen-year-old activist seriously. He answered,
"The same way you take a four-year-old boy preacher
seriously." I was committed to the cause and had been
for years. These men understood my dedication and
responded in kind. In order to get my youth organization off the ground, however, I knew I needed some
on-the-ground help. I needed a world-class strategist.

At the time, Bayard wasn't too popular with those
involved in Operation Breadbasket due to his increas-
ingly militant position on community issues in 1968;
he eventually became one of the United Federation of
Teachers' (UFT) most prominent Black supporters. (I
would later leave Operation Breadbasket myself due
to internal strife and the treatment of Reverend Jack-

son, who resigned while on a forced sixty-day suspension.) Because of his homosexuality, Bayard also wasn't very popular with the Black church. As such, our paths didn't cross so much as run parallel. Bayard's homosexuality didn't concern me. Frankly, I was more interested in hearing about how he organized marches and demonstrations. I knew he had learned from some of the best—A. Philip Randolph, who founded the Brotherhood of Sleeping Car Porters, the first Black labor union, and A. J. Muste, a former union organizer, among others—and everyone I spoke with said Bayard was by far the best organizer they'd known. If I was going to get my own youth organization off the ground, I'd need start-up advice from the man who knew it all.

I will never forget the day I met Bayard at his office. I remember standing outside, staring up at the New York City skyscraper, my heart full of excitement and my stomach a jumble of nerves. Inside, Bayard saw me immediately; I had come to him by referral from A. Philip Randolph, his mentor, who had been contacted in turn by my mentor Bishop Washington, who had vouched for me. I explained to Bayard what I wanted to do, and he peppered me with questions in that distinctive, almost proper-sounding voice of his: "What are your specific goals? Write them down. Number them. What's your strategy? Write it down." He spoke to me as if I was a grown man and not the teenager I was. I stumbled through my answers, and he elaborated on each one. Nearing the end of our meeting, he asked me the most important question of all: "How are you going to finance this?" I didn't have an answer for that; I was a teenager living with my mother, who was struggling to make ends meet herself. He called to his secretary, Rochelle Horowitz, and on the spot handed me a check for about five hundred dollars, my first contribution. I left that building standing a little taller than when I had entered it. A few weeks later, Bayard followed up with me, saying that he'd gotten Clarence Jones, a former advisor to Martin Luther King Jr., to host my first fundraiser in his apartment. It's impossible to say how my life trajectory would have been different had I not encountered Bayard. That's like saying without my having met James Brown, I wouldn't have known a father. Or without Jesse Jackson, I wouldn't have known how to structure my activism. Or without Barack Obama, John Lewis, or Elijah Cummings, I wouldn't have remained inspired. Bayard entered my life when I needed him most, and the early days of my own youth organization were indebted to his contribution, financial and advisory both.

Many years later, in 2017, I was invited to speak at the A. Philip Randolph Institute in Miami, Florida. During my speech, I let the audience know that the person who had founded their institute, Bayard Rustin, was the very same man who had gifted my youth organization with its first check. As I was leaving, an elderly white woman asked to speak with me privately. She looked to be in her eighties and had a kind of dignified bearing. She confessed to me that my story about Bayard was particularly meaningful to her.

"Why?" I asked.

"Because I'm Rochelle Horowitz. I wrote out that first check for you." I nearly fell over. It was as if I'd stepped backward in time and was once again standing in that sunlit office, Bayard's voice calling out her name. I remember I'd left that office feeling like a man. I stood outside on the sidewalk for some time, watching the traffic pass by and marveling at my good fortune. It was a moment I wanted to last forever, and it's probably why I still remember the address of Bayard's office—260 Park Avenue South. It was there that I took the first step toward becoming a leader of my own.

Bayard was active in the civil rights movement until his death in 1987, putting that fight ahead of his gay-rights activism. It's amazing to me that a Black gay man who helped usher in some of Black history's most significant legislative and policy changes, including the Civil Rights Act, and pushed forward an all-inclusive progressive agenda that addressed employment, housing, union, wealth distribution, and education, faced discrimination himself at every turn because of his sexuality. He was working for us, and yet the Black community was still slow to support gay rights. I wonder what Bayard could have done to advance the push for gay rights if he had focused his attention there. It was only late in his life, after the initial uprising of Stonewall, that he became a gay-rights icon. In a 1986 interview with Joseph Beam in the *Advocate*, Bayard said, "If we want to do away with the injustice to gays it will not be done because we get rid of the injustice to gays. It will be done because we are forwarding the effort for the elimination of injustice to all. And we will win the rights for gays, or Blacks, or Hispanics, or women within the context of whether we are fighting for all." He viewed one group's fight as everyone's battle, a sentiment largely missing in today's partisan politics. Yet, he also understood how his identity as a Black man went hand in hand with identifying as a gay man. In rare recordings released by Bayard's surviving partner, Walter Naegle, Bayard recounted an incident that helped him see how his identities informed one another, and why it was important to become a gay rights activist: while taking his place at the back of a segregated bus in 1940s Jim Crow South, a white child reached out for the ring necktie Bayard was wearing and pulled it. The child's mother said, "Don't touch a n*****." As Bayard saw it, that child was innocent of race relations and yet, if Bayard sat quietly in the bus, that same child would grow up thinking that Black folk don't mind sitting in the back of the bus or being called n*****. Bayard saw an opportunity, saying, "I owe it to that child that he should be educated to know that Blacks do not want to sit in the back, and therefore I should get arrested, letting all these white people know that I do not accept that." He continued, "It occurred to me shortly after that that it was an absolute necessity for me to declare homosexuality, because if I didn't I was a part of the prejudice. I was aiding and abetting the prejudice that was a part of the effort to destroy me."

In 2013, President Obama posthumously awarded Bayard the Presidential Medal of Freedom, the highest civilian award in the United States. In February 2020, Bayard was also posthumously pardoned by California governor Gavin Newsom. The governor also announced a clemency initiative that would help clear the records of other people who faced discriminatory charges for consensual sexual activity with people of the same sex.

THEN THEY CAME FOR ME

While the gay liberation struggle of the 1970s was a predominantly white, male-led movement, the incident that many say started it all—the Stonewall Uprising of 1969—was initiated by Marsha P. Johnson and Sylvia Rivera, two transgender women of color. Johnson was at Stonewall the night of June 28 to celebrate her twenty-fifth birthday. Rivera was part of the crowd that gathered outside as the police clashed with the bar's patrons and threw the first bottle. This was no ordinary bar fight; the patrons were tired of police harassment. Stonewall was one of the few places in the city where the LGBTQ community could gather and dance together without being arrested, but that balance was tipping and, in fighting back against police harassment, the patrons kicked off a social movement whose time had come. After Stonewall, members of the Mattachine Society, one of the earliest gay and lesbian organizations in the United States, split off to form the Gay Liberation Front, a more radical protest group. Other groups followed: Gay Activists Alliance, Radicalesbians, Street Transvestite Action Revolutionaries. Like Bayard, Johnson and Rivera helped spark a revolution that became a communal uprising. Being trans women of color, however, their efforts were largely marginalized by the larger gay community, and they, like so many others, were pushed to the fringe of the movement.

As a teenager, I was aware of Stonewall but only because of my sister: by the time she was eighteen, she was dragging me all over Greenwich Village—the heartland of New York's gay community—and while I have no recollection of it, she insists that I've been to the Stonewall Inn with her. I do remember going to Café Figaro and some other spots, but maybe because I was young, they were just restaurants and cafés to me. My activism back then was largely God-driven and focused on the immediate needs of the youth community in our Brooklyn neighborhood. In retrospect, I didn't see the connection, but I do now: the LGBTQ community and the Black community are fantastic allies because they're two different communities with real patterns of exclusion and immediate points of intersection. The most vulnerable members of the LGBTQ community, for example, are trans women of color who could benefit from the support of Black faith communities. In 2015, in recognition of LGBTQ History Month and National Coming Out Day, I formed NAN's LGBTQ Alliance, created to address issues like antiviolence, overpolicing, education, economic development, health and wellness, HIV/AIDS, and voter protections. I formed this faith-based initiative because I believe we have to be part of the movement forward. I don't believe anyone has the right to limit someone else's civil rights based on personal prejudgment or bias. Maybe it's my way of giving back to Bayard or paying it forward to new generations of the LGBTQ community.

I didn't participate in 1979's National March on Washington for Lesbian and Gay Rights but, by 1987, I was in full support of gay rights. In the early 1990s, I began to publicly show my support. I did so knowing I'd get pushback from the Black community and the church, which I did. The same thing had happened when I initially reached out to Bayard; several ministers expressed their displeasure with me. I didn't listen to them. The way I see it, I cannot in good faith preach civil rights for one group of people yet deny those same rights for another group. As Martin Niemöller expressed in his famous poem "First They Came," if you don't speak up in support of another group, who will speak up for you when there's no one left? If I started making excuses for my lack of support, how is that any different from a white Southerner back in the day who said, "Well, *I* don't have any problem with the Negroes. It's just that my boys won't understand." Or the guy in Bensonhurst who said, "Well, I didn't think it was right to keep Blacks out of the neighborhood, but everyone else on the block did, so I didn't say anything." You become what you claim to fight. I stand with the LGBTQ community, and I do so proudly.

ALL FOR ONE, ONE FOR ALL

Change doesn't come overnight, and as power shifts, we have to be careful not to bring our biases into the new paradigm. My argument with a lot of the so-called progressives is that they say they're racially inclusive but really aren't. Similarly, the Black community can't ignore the injustices faced by our Latino neighbors or the LGBTQ community at the risk of only fighting our own battles. It's one of the reasons I invited presidential candidate Pete Buttigieg to meet me for lunch at Sylvia's Restaurant in Harlem in 2019. I knew I'd get some flak for it, but it was important to me to make a point about intersectionalism. I can't fight for anyone unless I'm fighting for everyone. I brought Pete to the heart of Harlem just as I'd invited countless other politicians—Kamala Harris, Bernie Sanders, and Barack Obama when he was running. The former mayor of South Bend, Indiana, and I spoke openly about racism and homophobia, especially in the Black community and church.

I told Pete about my sister and how, when the issue of same-sex marriage became a national issue in 2000, she called me. Our conversation changed my thinking on the matter. She had asked me point-blank, "How are you going to deal with the question of same-sex marriage?" I told her I was supportive of people having partnerships. She pressed on in the way that only a sibling can do, not letting me off the hook. "But not marriage?" she asked. I answered her honestly, saying, "I don't know." She laced into me like she was the preacher, not me, saying, "Oh, that's moral. You're okay with gays living together, but they can't marry? Let me ask you something: If I dropped dead tomorrow, my partner shouldn't have the legal right to take care of my estate or have access to whatever we built together because you, a civil rights leader, say we can't be married? You've worked your whole life for social justice, but we're somehow not part of that equation? Is that how civil rights work?" She was right: if a civil rights issue is defined by whether someone, living in a civil society, faces discrimination of any kind, then the LGBTQ community falls under that umbrella definition. How could I stand for one without standing for everyone? I couldn't.

Pete and I spent our lunch talking about gay rights, but we also discussed policing issues in South Bend. At the time, Pete was still dealing with the repercussions from the excessive force used on and shooting of a fifty-four-year-old Black man, Eric Logan, by a white police officer in the South Bend police department. Pete would eventually go on to agree to an independent investigation by the Justice Department, but at the time he and I spoke, he was still reeling from the immediacy of the issue. I advised transparency and for him to be upfront and honest with the victim's family. The fact is, however, the policing problem in South Bend isn't unique to that city—too many Black communities all around the country are policed by majority-white police forces, who have little interest or investment in the communities they serve and often have a history of personal racial animus. Pete's political situation was especially touchy, however, because three months into his term as mayor, he ousted the city's first Black police chief, a sore spot for the Black community. Whether or not that back history played into the uproar around Eric Logan is moot: a Black man, again, was shot by a white officer, whose body camera was turned off. There cannot be, in any circumstance—local or national—even a casual acceptance of police misconduct. While we spoke about serious issues, our conversation itself wasn't difficult; I found him to be relatable and open-minded. The most "difficult" part of the meal may have been the throng of photographers who flanked the window, lights flashing. Apparently, we were a study in contrasts—on everything from our age, race, sexual orientation, and dining preferences. (I had toast, and he had the works.)

After our lunch, we held a joint press conference where Pete addressed the idea that America isn't ready for an openly gay president. That kind of rhetoric, he said, "gives America very little credit," and he was right. Obama confronted the same kind of thinking when he ran for the presidency. Hillary did, too. And in both cases, somewhere along the line, America turned a corner and cries of *We can't elect a Black president* turned to *Yes we can*. People should be judged on their merit, not by the color of their skin, their gender, or who they love. When the press conference was over and the photographers had dispersed, Pete did something I've never seen another politician do—and I've been taking presidential hopefuls to Sylvia's for years. He went back inside the restaurant and politely introduced himself to each table, shaking hands and talking. The atmosphere inside was amiable, with everyone calmly taking measure of this man, who listened earnestly and with the presence of an open heart, the cameras long gone. I realized then that Pete is someone who understands what it's like to be considered an outsider and yet, despite that or perhaps because of it, he's also comfortable in his own skin. I appreciate that authenticity.

GOD DOESN'T MAKE ANY MISTAKES

I've been a minister of several different congregations, and in each one, I'm usually confronted by a highly opinionated member of the congregation who wants to debate the merits of gay rights and their religious freedom. I say the same thing to each and every one of my concerned congregants: you don't have to have laws against people in order to protect your religious freedom. For example, there are certain Scriptural laws that are followed and maintained in the church that, outside the temple or the mosque, aren't federal law. It's one thing for a minister not to marry a same-sex couple because of the edicts of that particular religion. In this case, however, there's room for debate if a same-sex couple, as members of that particular religion, ask to be married by their minister; this is certainly a gray area where the minister must reconcile his or her teachings with the will of the congregants. The debate ends at City Hall, however, where no one can use their religion as a means to thwart state law. A marriage license isn't issued by the church; it's issued by the state. Every marriage is civil. You can't benefit from the public without deciding what part of the public benefits you. If you sincerely want to have your rights protected, an equal playing field for you and your loved ones, then you need to have that for everyone. No one needs your permission to be equal. Even with your religious conviction, no one needs you to sign off on their civil liberties.

Second to this discussion, I'm also invariably approached by an anxious mother or father seeking advice on or absolution for their gay child. I've given much thought to the matter. The best advice I can offer is this: if your child was born with a certain orientation, isn't it a matter for God to reconcile and not for you to decide whether or not that orientation is a sin against Him? Are you to judge that? Or are you to adjust to God's decision in creating your child to be who they are? Are we talking about your child, or are we talking about your own feelings—your possible embarrassment or shame? Your discomfort? If we're talking about the child, it's very basic: Do you believe they were born that way by God's hand or not? If we're talking about you, then let's wrestle with the fact that you may love yourself more than you love your child or God. If you love your child and can accept that God made them a certain way, then you can work on yourself. You can learn to forgive your weakness. You can find the strength in your heart to open it wide enough to let in the love. As Martin Luther King Jr. said, "I refuse to accept the view that manhood is so tragically bound to the starless midnight of racism and war that the bright daybreak of peace and brotherhood can never become a reality... I believe that unarmed truth and unconditional love will have the final word."

6

EVERY MAN IS YOUR BROTHER:

Immigration Control and Our Shared Humanity

Jesus was an immigrant. Born in Galilee, a region of north-ern Israel, we can most likely assume he was also a man of color and grew up in impoverished circumstances. God was his Father and, in His good grace, chose the Virgin Mary to bring Jesus into the world. Ask yourself: Of all the people in the world, why did God bring this person, this boy, into the world as His son? He could have selected a child of wealth or status. He could have chosen a Roman boy with lighter skin. Instead, Jesus hailed from squalid conditions, an impoverished social situation, and was subject to the Roman occupation governed by Herod, who sentenced infant males in Bethlehem to death. Why would God put His son in these circumstances other than to point out that there was something inherently wrong in this poverty, inequity, and cruelty? He did this so that His son could bring hope to the hopeless and inspire a people to rise up. According to Scripture, Jesus's parents fled with him to Egypt, further affirmation that he was probably a person of color; it would be nearly impossible to hide a Roman white child in dark Africa. If I was going to hide a Black child today, I wouldn't take him to Bel Air, California.

How can men and women of faith preach against refugees when Jesus was one himself? If Jesus's parents took him to Egypt to seek refuge, then, by definition, he's a refugee. It's a perversion of faith and the dogma of Christianity itself to espouse your personal religious beliefs when it's convenient for you, but to disavow its harder truths for your neighbor. In 1 John 4:20, it is written, "If a man say, I love God, and hateth his brother, he is a liar: for he that loveth not his brother whom he hath seen, how can he love God whom he hath not seen?" To put it bluntly: How can you love God whom you've never seen but hate your brother and sister who you see every day?

We employ a common refrain when our moral values don't match with the political expediency of the day: don't mix religion with politics. When I was a boy preacher in Brooklyn, some of the older ministers would admonish me with this advice, especially as I became more active in social justice. My response to them was the same: "When I preach to the congregation today, which Bible would you like me to use?" Encountering their puzzled faces, I'd explain, "Because the whole Bible is full of politics: the second book of the Bible details the exodus of slaves from an oppressive slave system, so I can't preach that. I can't preach Moses or Joshua. I can't talk about Pharaoh, Ebenezer, or the story of Daniel in the lions' den. Can't talk about David defeating the Philistines, how David's masterful slingshot helped him become king. There's not much left." The stories in the Bible aren't children's tales; they're stories that not only confront principled sin but also institutional and political sin, and whether or not God was protecting the children of Israel against such malfeasance. These are stories we need today more than ever, and to deny their truths means we're turning our back on valuable lessons, the wisdom of which can guide us out of our long, dark days.

In Matthew 19:24, Jesus says, "It is easier for a camel to go through the eye of a needle, than for a rich man to enter into the kingdom of God." To me, this is a direct confrontation of the political and the religious and wisely illustrates the politics of inequity. The immigrant and the refugee, along with other minority groups, have carried the weight of our systemic inequities on their backs and with their labor since the earliest days of this country's birth. The immigrant is especially vulnerable to exploitation, with many corporations using him for cheap labor, while today's unions simultaneously woo him for their organizational and political purposes; most unions bank on the idea that once an immigrant becomes a citizen, he'll vote for whomever the union endorses. He's used by both sides. If you're a person of faith, how do you practice religious humility and compassion—the lessons of which can be drawn from the immigrant's plight—and the importance of addressing such inequity while simultaneously bathing yourself in the opulence of someone like Trump and his gaudy, self-interested, empire/administration? How can we, as a country, be vested in that kind of political sin and turn our attention away from the poor migrant child, separated from his family, seeking refuge and kindness from a country whose political leader now deems him a criminal?

Before Trump had even set foot inside the White House, he had already trained his sights on demonizing the undocumented or illegal immigrant, popularizing the chant *Build the Wall* at his raucous campaign rallies. In promoting his so-called America First agenda, Trump has essentially departed from decades of a US immigration policy that centered on family reunification, asylum, and the safe harbor of refugees. What do we stand for today?

In his first week in office, President Trump issued two executive orders on border security and interior enforcement, and, working with the Pentagon, signed a third order restricting refugees and visa holders from Iran, Iraq, Sudan, Syria, Libya, Somalia, and Yemen. The countries listed for suspension of visas are Muslim-majority, while other countries that have experienced terrorism weren't listed. Saudi Arabia, for example, was excluded despite the fact that most of the 9/11 hijackers originated from that country. Is the Trump administration screening for possible terrorists, or is it targeting Muslim immigrants who practice Islam, the world's second-largest religion? All three executive orders contain fine print that undermine human rights—everything from limits of access to asylum and the expansive use of detention. In the ramp-up to the 2018 midterms, Trump politicized the caravans of Central American migrants traveling through Mexico to seek asylum in the United States, calling them an "invasion" and, in a tweet, blaming their efforts to seek refuge under the Democrats'—as he called them—"pathetic Immigration Laws!" According to a Gallup poll, immigration was one of the top issues for Republican voters heading into the election, thanks in large part to relentless, hyped-up coverage by Fox News and Trump's own inflammatory statements. For him, it didn't matter that the caravans disappeared from media coverage after the election or that they are primarily made up of women and children fleeing violence and not terrorists infiltrating cells from the Middle East. His rhetoric did what he wanted it to do: it criminalized the Other in racialized terms and stoked the fears and anxieties of his largely white Evangelical base. The link between immigration and crime is a unicorn—it's a myth, a figment of the American imagination. The majority of research on the subject has shown that there's no causal connection between immigration and crime in the United States. We could get into the weeds and dissect the statistics, or we can talk about the situation more broadly and from a moral perspective.

I believe that the United States has a moral responsibility to provide refuge to people who are legitimately fleeing oppression or life-threatening situations. I'm not calling for open borders, but we can clearly give refuge. I fail to see the difference in the humanity of the legal versus the illegal immigrant; I see the difference in deeming one type of immigrant illegal at one border and another immigrant legal at a different border despite the actions of both being roughly the same. We need one set of rules: equal protection under the law. The law shouldn't be based on where you're coming from; it should be based on how we, as Americans, want to be treated ourselves—with dignity, respect, and equal protection. That said, we need a uniform immigration policy for everyone, so the same policy we have at the Canadian border is also implemented at our southern border. Do we have a wall at the Canadian border? Why would we have one at the southern border? This talk about walls is caveman conversation and usually revolves around the idea of a porous drug trade, yet most drugs enter our country though existing ports of entry, and most of the people arrested for the smuggling are either US citizens or residents of the United States. The very idea of building a wall is antithetical to my religious beliefs. How can I preach about Jesus's life and the lessons he imparted while simultaneously ignoring the suffering of today's refugees, suffering that, at least in Central America, the United States had a destabilizing hand in for the past six decades? It's a moral paradox, one that puts me at odds with my own faith. I believe it's possible to welcome the modern-day refugee and care for the American citizen both; it's not a zero-sum proposition. It's not a moral question of whether we can accept the immigrant. The moral question is: How can we not?

Amadou Diallo:
The American Dream

The United States is a country comprised of immigrants. Throughout our history, we've experienced waves of immigration—from various countries—that have ebbed and flowed with each new administration and policy change. As of 2018, the nation's 44.74 million immigrants (legal and illegal) was the highest number in American history. Why do immigrants come to America? They come to escape persecution based on race, religion, nationality, or political opinion. They come to find refuge from conflict or violence or displacement due to environmental factors. They come for health care and to escape poverty. They come for more educational and economic opportunity both for themselves and their family, some of whom may already be citizens here.

In the 1990s, a young man came to this country seeking his stake in the American dream. At the time, his home country of Guinea was still reeling from years of unrest and mass killings under Ahmed Sékou Touré. This young man, eager in his pursuit of earning a computer science degree, cobbled together a life in New York City, working odd jobs and getting by. One night, after dinner, he came home to his apartment in the Bronx. Four plainclothes cops happened to drive by and, seeing him, believed he matched the physical description of a rape suspect from one year earlier. Standing in front of the vestibule of his building, the young man reached inside his pants pocket to withdraw his wallet for his ID. The officers fired a combined total of forty-one shots with semiautomatic weapons, nineteen of which hit the twenty-three-year-old immigrant. This kid, with nineteen bullets in him, had come to the United States believing he was going to find a better life. Land of the free, home of the brave.

A lifelong New Yorker, I grew up in the shadow of the Statue of Liberty. I look at Lady Liberty every day of my life, and, like most New Yorkers, have found inspiration and hope in Emma Lazarus's quote enshrined on her pedestal: "Give me your tired, your poor, your huddled masses yearning to breathe free." Those words are a sorry balm for Amadou Diallo's death. Those words—and the ideals they represent—fall short of Diallo's optimism. The last words he spoke to his mother were "Mom, I'm going to college."

New York's Guinean community mourned Amadou like he was their fallen son. Because many of them lacked legal papers, however, they had nowhere to go to express their outrage and hurt. The National Action Network organized a series of nonviolent demonstrations and marches, which led into thirteen days of civil disobedience. We started with nine protesters being arrested per day and, by the end of our period of disobedience, had over two hundred daily arrestees. I was arrested myself after blocking traffic at the intersection of Broadway and Wall Street, along with

Reverend Wyatt Tee Walker, former chief of staff for Martin Luther King Jr. and who, at the time, chaired NAN; Reverend W. Richardson, nationally acclaimed clergyman and member of our board; Reverend Herb Daughtry, a legendary New York activist; and six others. We protested the fact that the four officers had yet to be prosecuted. We protested the fact that then-mayor Rudolph Giuliani's approach to policing created an environment of fear and terror among immigrants and other communities of color. When the officers were acquitted, we didn't stop protesting. I personally met with Representative Charles Rangel and Deputy Attorney General Eric Holder to discuss an inquiry into the case by the Justice Department. The officers were eventually indicted in Albany.

I had been meeting with Amadou's mother, Kadiatou, an educated, big-hearted woman, who asked me to return to Guinea with her to help lay her son's body to rest. Throughout our meetings, I couldn't help but see myself through Kadiatou's eyes: I was an American whose country had betrayed her son. Was I any better than the four officers who killed him? As we travelled to Africa, my personal interrogation didn't stop there. My mind pressed on, flooding my thoughts with other questions I couldn't answer. How would the world find its peace with us? What do you say to the hundreds of people who thronged around our airplane in Guinea, ready to take back their son? What words do you offer the countless other immigrants who come to America each year, each day, eager to turn their dreams and hopes into reality? There was no justification for Amadou's death. All I could do was look into the face of his mother and promise her, like I've promised so many other Black mothers in America, that I would fight for justice. I would fight in the name of her son. I would redress my country's betrayal, and I would do so with heartfelt conviction. In news reports following his death, Amadou was often referred to as a West African street vendor—as if this status somehow explained or excused his mistreatment. The truth was Amadou was saving money for college. He came from an affluent family and spoke five languages. He wanted to make it in the world on his own. Years later, in an interview with Spectrum News NY1, his mother addressed her son's dreams, saying Amadou "believed in America.... If he was alive today, I know he would be a parent, he would be an entrepreneur. He would be helping people." As if to carry out her son's good intentions, Kadiatou was inspired to activism after her son's death.

How do we instill hope in the world that America is still a good, decent, and safe place when horrible things happen here to the very people we welcome—the tired, the poor, and the huddled masses? It's important to never forget that America is a unique democracy. We have the freedom to redress our past violations, our mistakes, and we do time and time again. The trick is learning from these mistakes so history doesn't repeat itself. It's also important that the various communities of immigrants form coalitions with other communities because it's only by mobilizing the combined efforts of our allies and voices that true change happens.

THE FABRIC OF AMERICA

There are those in this country who want to embrace a fantasy; namely, that the United States came into being by itself or of its own accord and not on the backs of the slaves and immigrants who were forced into labor to build it. This idea is the ultimate expression of white supremacist thought. And let's not forget the many Native American peoples whose lives and livelihoods were effectively snuffed out in the name of progress and expansion. We became the most powerful and wealthy nation in the world because we exploited other countries and people of color for their free labor. We can't undo this past, but let's acknowledge and compensate for it. Whenever I express this sentiment, I'm often besieged by a counterargument. "But Rev, what about the poor whites in this country? The Forgotten Americans? Don't they come before the immigrant?"

Many of the white working poor understandably feel abandoned, marginalized, and left behind. Many of the stable jobs for this sector have moved overseas. Unions aren't as strong as they used to be. The immigrant is a source of cheap labor. The Democratic Party has favored progressive agendas and social programs geared toward lifting the historically marginalized while ignoring the widespread struggle of the average farmer in Kentucky or the coal miner in Appalachia, people who once enjoyed the country's riches by virtue of their hard work. The world has changed and is changing still: job retraining programs that should have happened in the shift to a more global, tech-based economy didn't reach the farmlands or the coal mines. In the absence of programs and jobs engineered for this sector of our population, Trump stepped in and spoke to them directly, channeling their resentment and pain toward predictable scapegoats. But he's given them poisoned Kool-Aid. He's working for his friends, the wealthy and the corporations he favors, and telling the white working class that he's going to make American great again—a phrase that telegraphs some sort of magical time machine. He's going to take America back to the time when the manufacturing jobs of the white working male could provide for the whole family, when white America, by virtue of its whiteness alone, granted privilege, job stability, and economic freedom. I am telling you that world no longer exists, and it wasn't so great for a vast majority of the population anyway, including women, minorities, and the LGBTQ community, among others. Even if whiteness may provide some sheltered status in a racialized world, the white underclass is still poor—especially today—and I can assure you, poverty never feels great.

Of the eleven former states that belonged to the Confederate States of America, Virginia was the only one to vote Democratic in the 2016 election. It went from being a deep red state to solid blue, in part because of a change in population demographics, a shift that's happening around other parts of the country, too. Today, Virginia is home to a diverse group of people—one in ten people eligible to vote in the state in 2016 were born outside of the United States. In 1990, one in twenty-eight were foreign-born. In the wake of this changing demographic, the state government pushed through legislation to remove Confederate statues—statues that glorified Jim Crow—as well as to prevent hate crimes and ban assault weapons. These are the kind of commonsense changes that represent democracy at its finest: in removing its statues, Virginia is reckoning with the dark stain of past injustices inflicted on its Black and brown citizens. In preventing hate crimes and banning assault weapons, the good people of Virginia are saying that the safety of all its residents is a priority. This is the kind of pragmatic, commonsense decision-making that reflects the reality of our changing world, while maintaining the value structure of our democracy.

America is a better version of itself when we accept and celebrate diverse cultures. When we understand and embrace other parts of the world, we enrich ourselves. We open ourselves to possibility and discover other ways of doing things, mindsets, and worldviews different from our own. It helps us avoid the trap of becoming homogenous, with a universal, one-size-fits-all mentality. A closed mindset doesn't position us as a global leader; it isolates us further. That said, the word *diversity* has been cheapened over the years. Its meaning has become an advertising buzzword, a corporate box to check. Without the work that comes with truly understanding and integrating a different culture into the fabric of who we are, diversity means nothing. When woven together in a meaningful way, however, these distinct cultural threads make up America. We are both the weaver and the fabric itself. People shouldn't have to deny who they are in order to fit in. Instead, when we integrate everyone into the fabric of our society, we see that our distinct characteristics often complement one another, and whatever differences we have can hopefully be sorted out with reason, empathy, and compassion, and by relying on our shared democratic values and moral principles.

WE'RE NOT THE ENEMY

Immigration was one area where I disagreed with Obama's policies. I felt that his efforts to control and help stem some of the immigration crises at our borders were handled more as an issue of enforcement rather than one of real humanitarian need; he has one of the highest numbers of deportations in presidential history. That said, I was initially supportive of some of the policies he put in place to help alleviate the need for immigrants to come to the United States—he didn't deny access in the US, for example, to minorities and asylum seekers, but he did tighten vetting in response to terrorist threats. I support DACA, which would shield about 800,000 undocumented immigrants from deportation who were brought to the US as children and, as adults, largely contribute to the fabric of his country. His immigration policy also eliminated large work-site raids, which had been widely used in the Bush administration, expanded screening processes, and called for a reexamination of thousands of Iraqis who had already been admitted into the United States. While Obama's administration did separate families, it wasn't a common practice, and if minors were housed in separate facilities, it was mainly because they had already arrived at the border unaccompanied.

The difference between the Trump and Obama administrations with regard to immigration is largely one of tone and the severity of treatment: at no time did the Obama administration use rhetoric to dehumanize immigrants or make light of their struggles, and at no time were children locked in cages, their very existence criminalized. It's one thing for me to disagree with enforcement policies. It's another to have to debate the humanity of a five-year-old child deemed a future criminal, an enemy, by the current administration. Trump has essentially rendered these children hostages in his cruel political agenda. In fact, cruelty seems to be the name of the game, with Trump tweeting on July 3, 2019: "If illegal immigrants are unhappy with the conditions in the quickly built or refitted detention center, just tell them not to come. All problems solved!" The *conditions* of which he spoke include dangerous overcrowding, inadequate supplies like soap and toothpaste, and, in some centers, nowhere for the detainees to wash their hands or shower. Some children sleep on concrete floors in cages. The administration objected to the word *cage*, preferring the less offensive terms *pen* or *detention center*. Do you think children can tell the difference between a cage and a chain-link pen? Do you think semantics matter to them? The reason words matter all of a sudden to Trump and to Border Patrol is because they object to the *image* of people—children—being treated as animals, and yet they have no objection to the treatment itself, which speaks more to their lack of moral character than it does to any child's potential criminality. Under Trump's "zero tolerance" policy, over 2,300 families have been separated. To date, many children have yet to be reunited with their parents due to ineffective identification and registration processes.

In June of 2018, Attorney General Jeff Sessions used the Bible to defend the federal government's right to prosecute everyone who crosses the border illegally, quoting Romans 13: "I would cite to you apostle Paul and his clear and wise command in Romans 13, to obey the laws of government because God has ordained the government for his purposes." When I heard the attorney general quote the Bible out of context, using Scripture that's historically been a go-to line by proslavery Southerners to justify slavery and by Loyalists who opposed the American Revolution, all in the name of brown children being locked in cages, I knew it was time for me to go to Texas. (Outside of the United States, the same Scripture passage has been used to defend Nazi rule and to defend apartheid.) I think much of the motivation and the impetus to control immigration hinges on racism—I've not seen white babies at the Canadian border put in cages, have you?—and Sessions's use of Romans 13 was a lame game of connect the dots. Whether the administration uses mass deportation and immigration law or mass incarceration and street law—the border in the criminal-justice system being the court—to protect its whiteness, it's the same attitude of law enforcement across the board: the rules change depending on the neighborhood of the crime or the skin color of the person being arrested or deported. The impetus to control these populations or "infestations," as Trump has called them, is the same impetus used to historically defend and protect white supremacy.

Later that same month, Rabbi Jonah Dov Presner, who serves as the director of the Religious Action Center of Reform, invited me to be part of a delegation of faith leaders who were planning to stage a protest at the detention center in McAllen, Texas. We weren't the only faith leaders speaking out against the administration's immigration policy. Sessions's own church, the United Methodist Church, was aghast, with Reverend Susan Henry-Crowe, the church's general secretary, describing the administration's policies a "shocking violation of the spirit of the Gospel." My fellow travelers comprised ten rabbis from all four major Jewish religious movements, as well as prominent Catholic, Protestant, and Muslim leaders, about forty of us altogether. By the time we arrived at the detention center, more than two thousand children had been separated from their parents since the policy was instituted in early May. As of 2019, that number had swelled to 5,400, according to the American Civil Liberties Union. Authorities wouldn't let us into the actual facilities, and so we protested and held a vigil on the grounds outside. The day that we arrived was especially meaningful because it was only two days after the celebration of Juneteenth, the American holiday that commemorates the June 19, 1865, announcement of the abolition of slavery in Texas. (The Emancipation Proclamation of 1863 wasn't enforced in Texas until after the Confederacy collapsed.) As we spoke to many of the border-control workers, I couldn't help but think of America's ancestors—white and Black and everyone in between—who had been party to other family separations over our long history. I thought of the generations of Black families who had been torn apart. While I'm not a refugee from a third-world country, I might have been. I understand how the breakdown of a family, extreme poverty, and an uncertain future can wreak havoc on the psyche of a child, can destroy the parents' dreams of a better life. What are we—a country run by adults who should know better—doing to the psyches of the children clustered at our borders? When we lose our humanity, we lose the best of America. These children aren't the enemy. They're the expansion.

UNDOCUMENTED FEARS

The fears and anxieties surrounding COVID-19 and its economic fallout are unprecedented. Among migrants and legal and illegal immigrants, the stakes are especially high, with many concerned about possible deportation when seeking medical treatment. For many large, intergenerational, cohabitating immigrant families, social distancing is a luxury they can't afford...so is health insurance. According to a report by the Kaiser Family Foundation, among all immigrants, 23 percent of those who are lawfully in the country and 45 percent of those who are undocumented lack health insurance. Some immigrants who lack health insurance fear that visiting a health clinic may endanger their chances of getting a green card under the Trump administration's strict public assistance regulations. Others fear getting swept up by Immigration and Customs Enforcement (ICE). Low-income immigrant workers can't afford to take time off work, and most hourly gigs don't have sick leave, so it's either risk exposure or risk the paycheck: your life or your money. And let's be honest here: increased exposure for the immigrant worker means everyone's at risk. As of April 2020, ICE classified medical facilities as *sensitive locations*, where enforcement is avoided. Exceptions can be made, however, and for many immigrants, these exceptions are seen to be the rule under the Trump administration, making it nearly impossible for them to entrust the government and the mainstream medical community with their lives.

Perhaps realizing that containment may be the fastest way to increase the risk of contagion, the current administration began to release some of the forty thousand adults and children being detained across the country on civil-immigration charges, prioritizing those over sixty and pregnant women. Out of that staggering number of detainees, 600 were identified as vulnerable and 160 have been released as of March 2020. ICE has continued to make arrests during the outbreak of the pandemic. Pandemic or not, I believe ICE is in need of a major overhaul: it's been weaponized in such a way that it's more a bogeyman than an efficient or effective enforcement agency. It needs to be replaced with a different type of agency with a revised mission statement and message, one that doesn't rely on fear and intimidation and can adjust its mission during a pandemic. In the midst of a global health crisis, our collective response should be one that transcends language and cultural differences. Our response should be based on empathy for our fellow man and in recognition of our shared humanity.

COUNT ME IN

The end goal here of all of Trump's hateful rhetoric and immigration scare tactics is the suppression of the immigrants' collective voice and vote. Studies show that the more people there are who vote, the more the voting swings Democrat. The Obama administration understood this and did a lot of voter outreach and advertising, encouraging people to vote, targeting neighborhoods of color, and using Black- and Latino-backed radio shows to get the word out. The Trump administration, by contrast, sought to add a citizenship question to the census in a bid, it said, to help enforce the Voting Rights Act. It's been estimated that adding the citizenship question would reduce response rates among households with noncitizens by more than 5 percent. As the basis for deciding the number of representatives each state gets in Congress and how $650 billion in federal funds are distributed, the census is as important as any legislative mechanism we have. The Justice Department has other means of getting citizenship data—this citizenship question was just a low-down, dirty trick to undercount immigrant, minority, and low-income populations. The administration was forced to drop the issue after being blocked by the Supreme Court. It was a rare moment of victory in an onslaught of four years of the Supreme Court falling under its conservative sway, and one that's temporary at best. Make no mistake about it: the conservative justices on the Supreme Court didn't vote with their conscience or their morality. The administration had simply botched its legal approach so badly, they were forced to acknowledge the lack of legal standards. It's a victory nonetheless, and I'll take it. Every morning and every night, I get on my knees and pray. I pray for my loved ones—my children and my grandson— and then I pray for Ruth Bader Ginsburg, and in that order. Unfortunately, even RBG can't negate the fact that since Trump's been in office, he's confirmed 187 judges for lifetime appointments, which means that even if a Democrat secures the office of the president, the judicial landscape has already changed across the country. It will take decades to balance the federal courts.

Failing to add the question of citizenship to the census, Trump leaned on ICE, counting on it to apply the pressure and intimidation on minority communities to keep them out of the voting booth. If you think this is a craven attempt to rewrite the goals a country who once welcomed your tired, your poor, and your huddled masses, you're correct. But it doesn't end there. The Republicans of the good state of Wisconsin recently blocked absentee voting for the state's election primary during a global pandemic because they knew Democratic turnout would be low. We are fighting with our lives. This isn't a drill. This is what democracy looks like on life support.

I've seen a lot of these moves before. They're a consistent part of the political playbook. The characters aren't as startling to me because I know what came before: people like George Wallace, Jessie Helms, and Strom Thurmond. Even Bernie Sanders, as progressive as he is, dovetails into the policies of George McGovern. McGovern was a progressive in 1972, but he had problems dealing with Shirley Chisholm, and that informs some of how I perceive the progressive party today as not having fully reconciled itself to the needs of this country's Black and brown voters. Listen, the fact that we've been here before is both heartening and deeply disconcerting. I say to you, the reader, yes, we've confronted racism and xenophobia before, and in many instances, it's been worse. If history shows us anything, it's that we rise up. We are a country of tree-shakers. When someone asks me if I stand for the immigrant, it's the same as asking me whether or not I stand with Jesus. Whether it's my religious faith that's being recorded for posterity or my faith in the democratic process, I say, "Count me in."

7

HARD TRUTHS:

Climate Change, Environmental Racism, and Our Global Responsibility

As far back as the 1830s, local industry—lumber and paper mills, chemical processing plants, and automobile manufacturers—used Michigan's Flint River as a dumping ground for their waste. In the 1950s, the city of Flint switched to drawing its drinking water from a nearby reservoir because the river was so polluted, and in 1967, it began purchasing clean water from Detroit, which drew directly from Lake Huron. In 2014, after years of economic downturn, the city faced a $25-million deficit, and state and local officials returned to using the Flint River, a water source known for its history of pollutants. The move was intended as a cost-saving measure for the economically depressed, majority-Black city. It didn't take long for residents to complain about the water's color—cloudy yellow to a rust-red—as well as its odor and taste. While residents reported skin rashes and a General Motors plant stopped using the municipal water because it corroded car parts, government officials declared, "Flint water is safe to drink."

LeeAnne Walters, a stay-at-home mother of four, wasn't buying it. Besides her youngest daughters getting rashes, her fourteen-year-old son fell ill, not to mention she and her other daughter were losing clumps of their hair in the shower. Drinking water at her home showed 104 parts per billion (ppb) of lead, an unprecedented level. The US Environmental Protection Agency (EPA) action level for lead is 15 ppb, and the level for the World Health Organization (WHO) is 10 ppb. By federal law, officials were required to alert Flint residents of the health hazards immediately, but they didn't. Subsequent testing of the drinking water in other homes around the city, an effort largely spearheaded by Walters, showed E. coli in the water supply and dangerously high levels of lead—anywhere from 200 ppb to 13,200 ppb—known to cause serious health problems, especially in children. All the while, state regulators kept insisting the water was fine. In 2015, Flint officials fessed up, and the dominoes began to fall. In short order, Dan Wyant, the director of the state environment agency, resigned, the city declared an emergency, President Obama allowed the Federal Emergency Management Agency (FEMA) to provide $5 million in aid, and the Michigan House approved $28 million to assist the city. At the height of the crisis, and with the glare of the national media on the city, the National Guard distributed free bottled water and filters.

I first heard about the water crisis in Flint from Reverend Charles Williams II, a pastor of King Solomon, a historical Baptist church in Detroit, and the head of the Michigan chapter of the National Action Network. I've known Charles for years, having met him during my 2004 run for president when he was still a teenager. He served as a college organizer for my campaign later that same year. In some respects, he reminds me a bit of myself: passionate for social justice and deeply aligned with his religious calling. Charles told me about the tainted water in Flint before it hit national news. He wasn't the only person raising his voice and waving his arms, though. The good people of Flint had been sounding the alarm for a while, calling their city leaders, and telling them that their children were getting sick and, no, the water wasn't fine. The problem wasn't with the truth-tellers; it was with the power brokers, those politicians and state officials who ignored, dismissed, and denied the truth. Partnering with NAN, Charles helped publicize the issue on the radio, led on-the-ground efforts and rallies even as late as 2018, and to this day, he's still highlighting the water problems residents are battling—several years after the city's initial crisis. It will be several more before studies can show how drinking, bathing in, and washing with lead-tainted Flint River water has affected the development of thousands of children. I don't know what bothers me most: the fact that the government's initial response was so slow or that the public's attention was so fickle. The crisis blew up, and then the media turned its attention elsewhere, seemingly forgetting Flint overnight. How is it that we, as a country, can be at ease—comfortable, even—with ignoring the fact that our fellow Americans are drinking poisoned water? What if terrorists were poisoning our water? Would we sit up and take notice then?

While it's necessary to hold politicians accountable for their lack of action, it's also important that we look at our history as a country that recklessly contaminates and rarely holds large corporations, industries, lobbyists, or, for that matter, ourselves responsible in any meaningful way for polluting our waters, skies, and lands. Decades before Flint's automobile industry collapsed and long before state officials resigned over their botched efforts to mitigate a public health crisis, corporations were dumping toxic waste into a shared water system, all in the name of profit. Maybe they didn't know better in 1830. But we do in 2020, and it's happening still—and not just in Flint, but in other cities, too, like Newark, New Jersey. The fact that we can be relaxed about the issue of environmental injustice is part of a larger global problem, one that revolves around environmental racism. It's not always clear, but the way we view racial and income inequalities influences how we understand and respond to environmental injustice both domestically and abroad.

A GROUNDSWELL OF RESISTANCE

We like to think that the water crisis in Flint is unique to the American story. Unfortunately, it's part of a larger pattern, one that goes hand in hand with economic devastation. The city suffered massive economic disaster when the automotive industry declined in the middle of the twentieth century. A loss of factory jobs also meant a loss of residents. Those who could get out of Flint did, leaving behind a hollowed-out city, a pattern we've seen repeated across the country in similar struggling towns and cities, to devastating economic effect. Whereas economic devastation may come with the loss of industry and factory jobs, the hard truth about Flint—and other majority-Black and -brown cities—is that study after study shows that race, not income, is the number one indicator for the placement of toxic facilities in the United States. So, a factory may disappear and the town may be hurting, but the toxic waste of that factory is most likely funneled away from white neighborhoods and into gerrymandered districts of color. Case in point: Belews Creek.

Much of the pollution from North Carolina's coal-powered electrical plants is absorbed by Belews Creek, a predominantly Black community in a predominantly white county, the toxicity seeping into surface water and the surrounding connected groundwater that services the area. The heavy metals in coal ash include arsenic and lead, which contribute to nervous system and reproductive problems and cancer. Under the Trump administration, the EPA overhauled Obama-era regulations on coal-ash disposal and weakened rules on air pollution from coal-powered plants, changes that are estimated to result in premature deaths and widespread health issues. Belews Creek and Flint are just two examples of environmental racism. Every county in every state has a similar tale. People of color—not only in the United States but also around the globe—experience disproportionate exposure to climate change, pollutants, and toxicity. Poor Black and brown communities don't deserve a lesser quality of water, air, or land because of the color of their skin or their income level. It's a grim reality that those who are the least responsible for environmental toxicity and the subsequent effects of climate change often suffer its most dire consequences and are forced, again and again, to rise up and voice the injustice to them. North Carolina may seem an unlikely birthplace for the environmental-justice movement, and yet it was there that the direct-action work of the civil rights movement first gained traction in the fight against environmental racism, a term that itself only became clear during the Afton, Warren County, protests of 1982.

In the late 1970s, a man named Robert J. Burns, along with his associate, Robert "Buck" Ward, of the Ward Transformer Company in Raleigh, North Carolina, were looking to get rid of thirty-one thousand gallons of PCB-contaminated oil. (Polychlorinated biphenyls, or PCBs, are chemicals used as coolant fluids in all sorts of electrical appliances.) Both men were involved in a scheme to dump the oil, which was dripped along the highway shoulders of approximately fourteen counties. Ward, who did the dumping along with his son, was found guilty of violating federal law. Looking for a place to dump over fifty thousand tons of contaminated soil, EPA and state officials settled on the poor, rural, and 69 percent Black community of Afton in Warren County. The people of Warren County had other thoughts, however. Using some of the same tactics employed in the civil rights movement—marches, petitions, rallies, coalition-building, litigation, and nonviolent action—the people protested. Prominent civil rights leaders, like Reverend Ben Chavis and Reverend Joseph Lowery, of the Southern Christian Leadership Conferences (SCLC), and Reverend Leon White of the United Church of Christ's Commission for Racial Justice, joined in and helped publicize the idea that the environmental injustice of Warren County wasn't isolated. It was as much a civil rights issue as Martin Luther King Jr.'s 1968 strike was for sanitation workers in Memphis, Tennessee. The Warren County protests lasted six weeks and marked the first time in American history that citizens were arrested trying to stop the creation of a landfill. Some protesters literally put their bodies on the line and lay on the highway in front of truckloads of contaminated soil. Approximately 550 people were arrested. Their efforts, however, didn't prevent the onslaught of the trucks; the toxic waste was eventually deposited in the landfill. But people around the country took notice, and the people of Afton didn't give up, mounting multiple protests and direct-action campaigns against Governor Hunt throughout his terms in office. In 2004, and at a cost of $17.1 million, North Carolina finally detoxified the site completely.

Perhaps it should come as little surprise that the direct-action work of the civil rights found expression in the environmental-justice movement of Warren County. North Carolina has a long history of seminal protests, including in 1960, when four young, Black college students—the so-called Greensboro Four—staged a sit-in at a Woolworth's counter in Greensboro. Their protest helped ignite a movement to desegregate restaurants across the South. For as much toxicity and pollutants that exist in the American system, the spirit of resistance is in our groundwater, too.

REAP WHAT YOU SOW

In 2015, I was invited to speak at the White House Champions of Change, an event honoring twelve people of faith for their grassroots efforts in protecting our environment and communities from the effects of climate change. The honorees addressed the moral and social-justice implications of climate change; their combined voices were a clarion for active hope and spoke to the moral obligation faith leaders have in helping to protect God's greatest gift, Earth. Beyond this, however, we also have a moral obligation to call out injustice. Make no mistake: climate change *is* a civil rights issue. Unfortunately, with today's unprecedented hurricanes, fires, and rising temperatures, it's also an issue of Biblical proportion. Sadly, we've seen time and time again what happens when record-breaking storms hit disenfranchised communities of color.

In 2005, the Bush administration was slow to respond to the devastation of Hurricane Katrina in New Orleans, Louisiana, despite the fact that it was the strongest hurricane ever recorded on the Gulf. The city lacked any real evacuation plan, communities of color were displaced, and residents were largely left to fend for themselves. Many who lost their lives were living in the lowest-income areas of the city; the mortality rate among Black adults was 1.7 to 4 times higher than that of white adults. We saw a repeat—same plot, different setting—in 2017, when Hurricane Maria, the tenth-most intense Atlantic hurricane on record, plunged Puerto Rico's 3.4 million residents into a humanitarian crisis, knocking out electricity and water in large parts of the territory, ultimately resulting in a total infrastructure breakdown and the deaths of over three thousand people. A commonwealth of the United States, Puerto Rico was still recuperating from a twelve-year economic recession when the storm hit. The absence of government help in the immediate aftermath of the storm demonstrated both the Trump administration's lack of empathy and the corruption still plaguing politics and government agencies in Puerto Rico. If Puerto Rico was a white nation, I doubt President Trump would casually toss its hurricane survivors paper towels as he did when he visited San Juan's Calvary Chapel. Three years later, tens of thousands of hurricane survivors are still living outside and under tarps, and many farmers are struggling to replenish the local food. Locusts aren't raining from the sky, but with this much devastation, you'd be forgiven for waiting for the Plague of Darkness to descend. For many marginalized communities, climate change is a matter of life and death.

Wealthier nations, like the US, have created this global crisis: today, almost 50 percent of global emissions are produced by the richest 10 percent of the world's population. The wealthiest 20 percent are responsible for 70 percent. Around the world, indigenous communities are on the frontlines of climate change; they feel the impact of these emissions first and are often forced to relocate due to changing pressures like flooding, erosion, and food drought. According to a 2019 World Bank study, more than 150 million people from places like sub-Saharan Africa, South Asia, and Latin America will be displaced because of environmental stresses. Most climate refugees will leave their land behind to move into slums or overcrowded cities. Some, however, will try to find a better life somewhere else, leaving their homeland entirely. If politics were ruled by our sense of morals, these refugees would be given asylum, and environmental injustice would be rectified. Sadly, there are few heroes in politics. Instead, the countries responsible for the environmental stresses behind these large-scale global displacements are tightening their borders, and in the case of the Trump administration are literally shifting blame: in 2018, for example, just a year after the devastating fallout of Hurricane Maria in Puerto Rico, the Department of Homeland Security moved $10 million from FEMA, which is responsible for natural-disaster preparedness, to ICE to pay for migrant detention. To be sure, mass migrations are dependent on several factors—crime, sexual violence, poverty, unjust political systems—but climate disruption is only making the situation worse, especially as the world continues to heat up.

In Galatians 6:7, it is written, "Be not deceived; God is not mocked: for whatsoever a man soweth, that shall he also reap." Are we so blind to this simple truth? If we are, God is right to deliver all that we deserve.

Al Gore:
Ahead of the Times

In 1976, Congressman Al Gore held his first congressional hearing on climate change and cosponsored hearings on toxic waste and global warming. It was only four years prior that the UN held its first environment conference. Climate change, however, didn't factor into that first conference. The conversation, instead, revolved around chemical pollution, atomic bomb testing, and whaling. From the outset, Gore was always working ahead of the times. When the Intergovernmental Panel on Climate Change (IPCC) reported its first assessment report in 1992, Gore had already written a book on the subject, *Earth in the Balance: Ecology and the Human Spirit* and, in the same year, was chosen as Bill Clinton's running mate.

I met Vice President Gore several times during the late 1990s. While he and Clinton were part of the centrist movement of the Democratic Party and I was more progressive, I'd always gotten the impression that we were on different sides of the same coin. In 2000, when Gore made his run for the presidency, I called for a debate between him and Senator Bill Bradley of New Jersey at the Apollo Theatre. Gore was hesitant, viewing me as being too controversial a figure. His team decided that we would meet at his daughter's house to discuss the matter and air our differences in private.

When my SUV pulled up to his daughter's house, the press corps, who had been following Gore and was already camped on the lawn, saw me and started snapping photographs. So much for privacy. Gore greeted me warmly and welcomed me inside. After some social niceties, he dug in, asking me outright: "What do I tell Jewish voters, who are upset with you over Crown Heights, that I've agreed to your invitation to a debate?" I politely told him that those voters should read the full story about my involvement in Crown Heights, and it would become clear that I hadn't been there to incite riots. "But let me ask you a question," I said, turning the table. "What do I tell Black voters when you were running for president in 1988 and your chief supporter in New York was Mayor Ed Koch, who said, 'A Jew would be crazy to vote for Jesse Jackson'?" We agreed that our records spoke for themselves; we both had perceived baggage—fair or unfair—in our various communities. With our differences addressed, on February 21, 2000, Gore and Bradley took center stage at the historic Apollo Theatre, a venue more famously known as the place where Billie Holiday, Ella Fitzgerald, and Sarah Vaughan, among other legendary performers, got their start. It was the first time presidential candidates had a debate in Harlem.

I asked the first question of the evening: in light of the Amadou Diallo and Abner Louima cases, what concrete steps would the candidates take to keep crime down but at the same time confront the problem of police brutality and racial profiling? Gore responded by saying that the first civil rights act of the twenty-first century, should he be president, would be a national law outlawing racial profiling. The theater burst into applause. Over the course of the evening, the candidates debated everything from education vouchers and health care to reparations and the criminal-justice system. Only one question was raised on the subject of environmental justice. Audience member Peggy Shepard of West Harlem Environmental Action asked what kind of action each man would take to protect communities of color disproportionately impacted by pollution and the asthma epidemic. Gore's well-intentioned, if generic-sounding, answer could have been given by any one of the 2020 Democratic nominees. He said, in part, "I think we ought to have clean air and clean water, and we ought to have a president who's willing to fight for them. And incidentally, we can improve our economy and create millions of good new jobs, if we go about building the new technologies that can help clean up the environment." Hindsight is always twenty-twenty, but I often think back to that debate night. It pains me to think that Gore had better answers to questions I didn't even know to ask; few of us did.

Later that year, after Gore would win the popular vote but lose the electoral vote to George Bush, he would return to the issue of climate change, working on a slideshow that would eventually become the basis for his award-winning documentary *An Inconvenient Truth*. In his first one hundred days as president, Bush reversed a campaign promise to regulate carbon dioxide from coal-burning power plants. By the end of his term, Bush had deregulated key components of the Clean Water and Clean Air acts, protections of the Endangered Species Act, and reduced enforcement efforts in the EPA. Perhaps most damaging, however, the administration injected widespread doubt into the scientific facts and findings of climate change, something Trump has expanded upon for his own political and financial gain.

Several years later, Gore reached out to me to appear in a commercial along with Reverend Pat Robertson—my political opposite—for a global warming ad campaign sponsored by his organization, Alliance for Climate Protection. While Robertson and I have certainly had our political differences, he and I come from a similar background in terms of our faith. We were both brought up following the teachings of some of the same great ministers, men like Bishop J.O. Patterson and Bishop Charles Blake. Our pairing for the television ad was, of course, intentional and meant to show the world that if we could come together in the name of addressing climate change, everyone could. Speaker of the House Nancy Pelosi and former speaker Newt Gingrich also appeared together to deliver the same message. It's a message I believe to this day. We cannot address climate change as partisan players. Instead, we need a coordinated effort among all the nations of the world, men and women of every faith, ethnic, and racial background working together to formulate a compassionate and collective plan. Al Gore understood this from the start. He believed that the issue of climate change was one that could unite not only centrist and progressive Democrats but Republicans, too.

In all the time I knew Gore, I rarely saw him passionate or heated, with the exception of when the topic of climate change was raised. Only then did he truly operate on all cylinders. It was a remarkable transformation to behold: he could address every issue under the sun in his characteristic earnest and sober style, but when he spoke about global issues facing our future generations, the impact of corporate responsibility, and the need to protect our resources, he became someone else entirely—a visionary driven by a sense of justice and passion, yet still in possession of his signature staid and calm sense of logic. For him, climate change was *the* issue—not just in terms of the political world but also in terms of our everyday humanity. When he spoke about climate change, Gore was less like a politician and more like an activist, fired up.

Today, more than any other time in modern history, we have access to technological and weather-related data that scientifically prove beyond reasonable doubt that our planet is warming to temperatures that will soon make life prohibitive. To be able to harness such information at such a critical time in our planet's life is astounding. Unfortunately, we're also living during a time in which the current administration and others want to discount the progress of the human mind and dismiss the scientific facts on which climate change research is based. That we're even second-guessing reality and science—on-the-ground facts—is a defeat for the body politic. It's time for us to stop entertaining this kind of nonsense. The opposition is firm in their lies, and we are weak in our truths. The space between the two is wide enough for Trump to drive a Mack truck through it, and he does.

In January 2020, Gore delivered the closing remarks at the World Economic Forum in Davos, Switzerland, where he spoke about the urgency of climate change, saying, "This is Thermopylae. This is Agincourt. This is Dunkirk. This is the Battle of the Bulge. This is 9/11." His comments predated the administration's response to the COVID-19 outbreak in America, but we can apply some of the lessons learned during the pandemic outbreak to help coordinate international efforts to address climate change. In other words, we can start treating climate change as the real-life emergency Gore has been warning us it is.

THE NEW NORMAL AND THE GREEN NEW DEAL

The COVID-19 pandemic has laid bare, in more ways than one, just how fragile and interconnected our world is. Global social-distancing measures have impacted our seas, air, and land in unforeseen ways. With far fewer cars on the ground, planes in the sky, and cruise ships plowing the oceans, scientists have been able to study what happens when the world slows down. Under pandemic lockdown, satellites have recorded a massive decrease in the concentration of nitrogen dioxide in our atmosphere. Besides the atmosphere being less polluted, our airwaves are, too. Noise pollution has decreased, giving wildlife a break from the stress-inducing hormone levels that typically spike with lots of noise. Seismic activity is also down. A reprieve of a few months' worth of pollutants and noise level doesn't mean anything, however, if business and human activity resume at their prepandemic levels, but it is a small harbinger of what's possible if there's a united global effort to combat climate change. To be sure, the pandemic is an emergency, but it's also a once-in-a-century opportunity to examine how less human activity contributes to our natural world. In the face of the pandemic's multipronged and daunting crises—economic, health, social, political—perhaps there's a chance to build something better, a new normal that lays the foundation for a more robust, balanced, and harmonious future.

The COVID-19 pandemic has painfully illuminated the various problems and inequities of our country—everything from racial disparities in wealth and health to a lack in federal leadership. After the Great Depression, Franklin Delano Roosevelt instituted the New Deal, which was largely based on the idea that the government should help provide Americans with the means and freedom to create a stable life. There was a rush of policies and public investments, including the creation of Social Security and minimum wage laws, along with other helpful initiatives like bringing electricity to rural America, building low-wage housing in cities, and planting scores of trees in areas ravaged by the Dust Bowl. In his eleventh State of the Union Address, Roosevelt said, "We have come to a clear realization of the fact that true individual freedom cannot exist without economic security and independence… People who are hungry and out of a job are the stuff of which dictatorships are made." Today's unemployment rate has surpassed the levels of the Great Depression. To get the country back on track, we are going to need a sweeping plan.

The Green New Deal, while originally conceived to address the challenges of climate change and environmental injustice, draws much of its inspiration from Roosevelt's original proposal and may be both big enough in scope and flexible enough to tackle to some of the fundamental issues we'll face in the aftermath of COVID-19. The Green New Deal calls for a massive investment in renewable energy, energy efficiency, and clean transportation and would help workers transition from working in coal and high-carbon industries to green jobs. In a bid to help address some of our country's glaring socioeconomic inequities, it includes key components of a progressive framework: free universal health care, childcare, and higher education. We can debate its merits and details and adjust its goals to encompass the real-life needs of all Americans, but we need to start somewhere. With the goal of restoring economic security and equal opportunity to our citizens while simultaneously addressing the burning issue of climate change, the Green New Deal may be a place to start.

GOD'S COUNTRY

In the Bible, it is written in the Psalm of David 24:1: "The earth is the Lord's, and the fulness thereof, the world, and they that dwell therein." As a man of faith, I am moved to action to address the moral injustice of climate change. From a faith-based, moral perspective, how can I stand idly by as we blatantly debase God's gift? The way I see it, to do nothing in the face of climate change, you either don't believe God's gift is truly a gift—a mindset that in itself is a defilement—or you don't care and have sacrificed your moral code in the name of profit, political expediency, and to the sincere detriment of your brothers and sisters. I have a hard time trusting the moral character of any person—secular or religious—who supports an administration with a climate change denier at the helm, a man who willfully destroys our wetlands, rolls back environmental standards at a breakneck pace, and challenges basic science that even a child can understand and logically support. The Trump administration is deregulating the private sector to literally poison God's land.

What kind of world do we want to leave our children? Our grandchildren? The hard truth today is that kids on every continent of this planet are already living with the real-life, day-to-day effects of climate disruption. No matter where they live—from the pollution-choked city of Delhi to the Pacific Northwest, where massive fires have turned the sky red—this is a generation growing up with our collective failure to meaningfully address climate change. These threats aren't taking place somewhere in the distant future. They're happening right now. Scientists have warned us about the sixth mass extinction, but it's already here. A recent study published in *Nature* magazine shows that if greenhouse-gas emissions remain on current trajectories, abrupt collapses of wildlife and ecosystems in the oceans and tropical forests will begin in the next decade. Wildlife is not only dying out due to habitat destruction, overhunting, toxic pollution, and climate change, but our patterns of overconsumption—of everything from plastic straws and bags to excess amounts of meat and dairy—are accelerating the rates of mass extinction.

The true measure of any man is that he leaves the world better than the one he inherited. We used to believe this. Today, we seem not only content to turn our backs on God's creation but willing to sacrifice our children, too. To teach our children and grandchildren about the value of nature, to read them colorful picture books on the wonder of polar bears and the fragility of the coral reefs while we're simultaneously killing the beauty of what we preach and teach is the absolute height of moral hypocrisy and spiritual effacement. We've gone from being a culture that believed in the idea of personal sacrifice and service for the sake of our families and for the greater good of our neighborhoods and communities to being a nation that revolves around self-gratification and -indulgence, which only leads to further self-destruction. We celebrate this new kind of selfish mentality, assuming that once I get mine, the game is over, the rest don't matter anyway. It's easy to pass the buck. It's easy to say that climate change is bigger than you and me and, therefore, we're not personally responsible. It's easy to disregard hard science. But that doesn't make it right.

Scientists may say we're past the point of appealing to action for the sake of our children, but I'm not a scientist. They argue that none of our emotional pleas have yielded the kind of widespread, sweeping change needed to persuade the fossil fuel industry, the politicians, or their corporate underwriters to reverse global destruction. Obama tried, but unfortunately many of his policies and pieces of legislation are unraveling, as is our commitment to any global-climate pact. As recently as March 2020, for example, the Trump administration relaxed Obama-era automobile fuel-efficiency standards, allowing cars to emit nearly a billion tons more carbon dioxide than they would have under Obama's standards, effectively undoing the government's most substantial effort to combat climate change. Just because we've failed ourselves and failed our children doesn't mean the fight is over. In 1963, Martin Luther King Jr. delivered a speech in Detroit in which he famously said, "If a man hasn't found something he will die for, he isn't fit to live." I won't go so far as to say you need to die for something, but I will say you need to live for something. If you can't live for yourself, I'm asking you: live for your children. Because here's the deal: the children know better. They know that the world they've inherited is teetering on a knife's edge. Because they know there aren't enough adults in the room doing the work, some of them are rising up.

It's impossible to write about the issue of climate change and environmental injustice without writing about Greta Thunberg, the teenage Swedish environmental activist. I've never met Thunberg personally, but I recognize the fire in her belly, the way she says what she means and means what she says, even when the truth blunts. When Thunberg was eight years old, she began studying up on the world around her and was shocked by what she learned: if we stayed on course with our current rates of pollution and environmental destabilization, the earth would be radically, irrevocably different by the time she was an adult. Massive wildlife deaths, more catastrophic weather, mass migrations of environmental refugees, problems in the food chain, and everywhere pain, suffering, shock, and death. She quickly saw through the hypocrisy: Why should she attend school to prepare herself for a world that may not exist at all? Why prepare herself for adulthood when her very livelihood and that of her friends— her entire generation—was being sacrificed anyway? Why continue building the house when the house itself is on fire? In August 2018, Thunberg didn't attend school and camped out in front of Sweden's parliament with a handmade sign: *School Strike for the Climate.* Today, she's a leader of a movement, pushing against the tides for change. Gore may predate her, but Thunberg's message is delivered with an urgency no one can ignore. When she tells us our house is burning, we would be wise to start scrambling for our buckets of water.

8

HOW TO BE AN ACTIVIST:

Organizing, Using the Media, and Stirring Up Controversy

I've been an activist for most of my life. Along the way, I've been spat on, stabbed, and invited to formal state dinners. I've been up and I've been down, but I've never lost my way. My activism may have been a combination of the times, the need I saw in my community, and a result of the influence of the men in my life, pastors and leaders who inspired me to look at my station in life, and that of my neighbors, and call it as I saw it. My activism is also, of course, informed by my faith, but it isn't dependent on it. I've known several secular activists, men and women roused to action because injustice demands it, because to do nothing is worse than the injustice itself. I got in this game because I was angry—angry at the conditions of my childhood neighborhood, a place where ambulances were slow to show; angry at the mistreatment and threats I experienced daily simply for being a Black boy in America; angry at the institutions, industries, and power brokers who rigged the system for their benefit. I'm still angry, because things have gotten better but they haven't been fully rectified. Gains have been made—and lost—in the name of civil rights, but it's not enough to simply look after your own. Social justice requires equal opportunity for all, and until everyone is afforded the same rights, protections, and opportunities, my anger won't abate and my work won't be done.

I'm often approached by young activists or everyday, concerned citizens who want to know how to make a difference in the world. "How do I start a movement?" they ask. "What can I do to stop police brutality? To stem violence against women? To help migrant children?" Everywhere, people are asking the same fundamental questions: What can I do to be of service? To help? At the National Action Network, we've created seminars and tutorials to help give people the tools they need to both organize and maintain a movement. But to be of service and to make a difference in the world, you don't have to start a movement from the ground up. In fact, I think this should be done *only* if there's a vacuum in your community and no other functional or effective group already exists there.

If you want to become an organizer for your community, it's important that you first identify your priorities. What is it that you want to combat, confront, change, or engage? Is it health care, climate change, women's rights? Take your pick. In reading this book, were there particular subjects that inspired you to action? Which ones? Now, prioritize those causes that are the most meaningful to you. Activism without a clearly defined cause is a mob. Second, do your homework. What is the state of that cause or movement in your particular locale? Is there already an active organization addressing your concerns? Is it effective, or does it need help? If there's already an active and effective group, join it. If there isn't one, get a group of interested people together to form something of your own. Start small—three dedicated people is enough. The key word here is *dedicated*; you want people who care as much as you do about whatever cause it is you're advocating for. Third, contact your local officials. Don't start at the presidential level. Instead, reach out to your local council members to find out what their policies are. Where does the local leadership stand on the issue you're most interested in? Do they already have initiatives in place? Do they need assistance? Start building from the ground up. It doesn't take much to start a coalition; the trick is in sustaining it.

Make sure you're registered to vote, and attend the local town meetings. Become a presence in your own neighborhood and at your children's schools. Participate in city council meetings, town halls, and community board meetings where you can begin to raise issues. Don't even think about local or social media until you're connected in the actual community where you want to make a difference. You must be embedded in your environment in order to change it. Activism doesn't benefit from a top-down approach where you parachute in, ready to save the day, like a superhero or a so-called latte liberal. You must build from the ground up and be part of the community—the churches, the civic groups, the volunteer organizations—you want to mobilize. If you don't have a strong backing, it's easy for your opposition to turn you into a threat to the very community you want to change. And if you're branded a threat, the opposition can discount whatever it is you're working toward. Listen, there's no such thing as a change agent who won't be tested. If your opposition doesn't come after you, then you're not effecting real change. The opposition can't disassemble you, however, if you're part of a cause that's bigger than yourself and built into the community. They may not like you at the PTA or the city council meeting, but after the third or fourth meeting, they'll be used to you being there. You may not be known in the church, but after a month or two, they're going to be glad you're there to help with the next bake sale. I can't stress this enough: be an active part of your community.

Once the movement begins to gain momentum, take a look at your personal vulnerabilities. I advise this from personal experience. Are your relationships in order? Do you have outstanding financial debts? Tie up any loose ends; the tighter you are, the better. Make no mistake about it, though: no matter how tight your operation is, the opposition will find a way to loosen you up either by your own undoing or someone else's.

Know the issues facing your community thoroughly, but more importantly, understand your opposition's points as well as you know your own. Don't be so lopsided that you get swiped off balance when the opposition attacks, using their key points as leverage against you. Activists can't live in a bubble, surrounded by people who share their thoughts on every matter. You must engage with people outside your comfort zone. You must respectfully engage with the opposition. You must keep an open mind at all times and speak with all people—really speak with them—to better understand their perspectives and why it is they believe what they do. If you're secure in your belief, you're not insecure in talking to people who may disagree with you. If all you're doing is speaking with people who already agree with you, you're not really secure in your thoughts. You're simply insulating yourself from the challenge of testing them out in the real world.

Lastly—and this is particularly difficult, I know—it's important to do a vanity test every once in a while. Speaking personally, sometimes my vanity outran my sanity, and I had to check myself. As you grow as an activist, it's tempting to think that you need to become the public face of whatever movement it is that you're leading, and in some cases, that's absolutely the right move. The question you need to answer is: Am I doing this next move, whatever that move may be, so that I can be seen? Or am I doing it because I believe it will help effect change? Maybe that means you turn down certain interviews or speaking engagements. As an example, I've hosted *Saturday Night Live* two times, the first in 2003 when I was running for president. At the time, my staff didn't want me to host, thinking it would turn me into a political sideshow. I decided to host the show anyway because I knew I needed to show the American public that I wasn't the terrifying figure the media painted me as. I needed to be able to effectively raise the issues of racism, criminal-justice reform, and policing to the mainstream, and *Saturday Night Live* gave me a great platform to help elevate and publicize my message. Plus, it never hurts to be able to laugh at yourself. A few years later, Rachel Noerdlinger, one of the country's most renowned publicists and longtime adviser to NAN, called to tell me that Trump wanted me to appear on *The Apprentice*. It was, in my mind, a perfect setup for Trump to tell me I was fired from whatever asinine challenge he'd issued. I said no. His team offered me more money, and Trump personally called me twice to get me to budge. Appearing on *The Apprentice* would have hurt the movement and issues I've dedicated myself to advancing. Over the years, I've learned the difference between being able to laugh at yourself (as on *SNL*) and being laughed at.

In life, you're measured as much by what you turn down as by what you accept. There's something strengthening about turning down an offer or an opportunity because you're holding yourself to a greater cause or standard; it fortifies you and keeps you grounded.

THE MEDIA

For an activist, knowing how to use the media, be it traditional—newspapers, magazines, radio, and television—or social is crucial. The backbone of any direct-action movement is visibility. We march so our voices can be heard, our bodies seen, the issue up front and center, demanding to be dealt with. The media, as much as it can be used as a weapon, is also a tool, and activists use it to apply pressure and put focus on a particular issue. Martin Luther King Jr. understood this. It's one of the reasons he went to Birmingham and Memphis, where he was killed. His teams were already doing direct-action work on the ground in both places, but he understood that his presence would bring media attention, and it did. The altercation between protesters and state troopers on the Edmund Pettus Bridge in Selma was filmed and broadcast into Americans' homes on the same day it happened; that changed the dialogue and focused the public's attention. The media can make or break a standoff.

People call NAN when injustice demands an audience. A grieving family or community rises up to say *enough*. It's the job—the responsibility, even—of an activist to telegraph injustice and force its public reckoning. People frequently lobby the complaint that all I want is publicity. That's exactly right. No one calls me to keep a secret. They call me to shine a light on an issue, which helps build the social-justice movement. That said, it's easy to conflate celebrity status—and the limelight—with being an activist. I've found that young activists are particularly vulnerable to this confusion, in part because so much of youth culture today revolves around being your own so-called brand and getting eyeballs on social media. Listen, I get it. I, perhaps more than most, understand this confusion because I've struggled with it myself. In the age of Trump, too, it's easy to conflate celebrity status with power. An activist is active because he or she wants to deal with the needs of people directly and to give voice to those who are most vulnerable. Some activists become the recognizable face of a movement. For those who like the limelight, this may be a personal perk and a strategy both. For others, it's a liability. I've been working as an activist since I was a teenager, and I've seen more people come and go because they get blinded by the light. The point of the light is to shine a spotlight on a problem, not to bask in it yourself. It's absolutely crucial you don't get in the way of your own cause.

Personalities die out *unless* they fill a vacuum or a need. Trump knows this better than anyone. The minute you believe that your charisma or personality is the thing that the people need, you've lost the movement.

CREATIVE TENSION AND CONTROVERSY

To be an activist, you must be comfortable with confrontation. It's a crucial organizing tool. It's a common problem, for example, to have competing visions among organizational groups within the same movement. No one understood this better than Martin Luther King Jr., who often presided over rival factions within his own organizations. By most accounts, he encouraged the airing of healthy disagreements, believing it was important to not only have every voice heard but also to debate the merits—the pros and the cons—of each perspective. He believed in the benefit of dealing with conflict, if not shying away from it, because it's only in the act of confronting someone else's beliefs and practices that we test and strengthen our own. Our life principles and values should be meaningful enough to feel justified and strong enough to withstand trials and tribulations. Our commitment to our most sacred values should be so strong that we're willing to base our lives on them—in extreme cases, even die for them. Martin Luther King Jr. called the act of engaging in discomfort—of confronting our disagreements head-on— "creative tension"; often the most forward-thinking ideas and revelatory insight occurs during these tense moments, when everything is on the line and challenged. You could call the past four years of the Trump administration the embodiment of King's principle. If you don't confront a problem, you will never solve it. You will never even see it as a problem.

People who work for social change are in the position of making people uncomfortable and in bringing comfort to those who have none. This is what happens when you shine a light on problems most people want to stay hidden. Most people try to find comfort in preassigned places. An activist, however, has to be intentional about pushing for change, no matter the discomfort it may cause. In fact, it's a good idea to train yourself to be intentional about exercising your own personal discomfort.

I work out at four in the morning each and every day. I don't take the easy route; I intentionally make myself uncomfortable. When something becomes too easy for me, I up the ante because the minute we challenge ourselves, we bring out the best in who we are. As a whole, we have to move out of our comfort zones in order to heal this country. Do not hide in your silo. Do not hide in your comfort zone. When you seal yourself off from the lessons learned by pushing yourself, you believe what other people tell you rather than thinking critically for yourself. Do not be afraid to engage in a problem or an issue more concretely. Yes, you will be called names. You will be called a rabble-rouser and an agitator. The opposition may try to weaponize your opinions and beliefs. It doesn't matter. Be active in your activism. Pursue a greater sense of understanding, compassion, and empathy.

To the critics who say I cause and have caused problems—whether in Howard Beach, Bensonhurst, Crown Heights, or wherever else—I say that I'm exposing the problem. I'm unapologetic in my actions working for change. I don't need the armchair analysis of a member of the intelligentsia to explain race relations to me when I know, simply from being a Black man in America, that if I go to Howard Beach to protest the killing of another Black man as I did in 1986, and I and my fellow protesters are pelted with racial slurs and watermelon rinds, something is deeply wrong with the state of our union. The problem has to be addressed, and no amount of smearing my name or digging up dirt on my personal mistakes or missteps or writing outrageous articles about me will make the systemic problem go away until it's confronted with equanimity, compassion, and a clearheaded yet direct approach. That said, I got to a certain point in my life where I no longer cared whether or not I stirred up controversy and discomfort. Each time I read a new outrageous headline about me, usually about how I was causing racial discomfort, I asked myself the question: Who exactly am I being controversial to? The newspaper executives who wouldn't allow Blacks to work in the newsrooms? People who barred Blacks from attending certain colleges? People who were offended by another Black boy's death? And I'm supposed to care about what they think about me? I'm supposed to curb my outrage because it's offensive to them and their sanctimonious status quo? I wouldn't be controversial if the situation itself lacked controversy.

I've noticed something about people who are easily offended: they usually operate in a system of unfairness and, more often than not, choose not to confront the unfairness or expose it even to themselves. Then they have the nerve to seek me out to gain their approval. This is delusion at its most insidious. It boggles the mind. Do they not see that their careful protection of the status quo is worse than lashings? I refuse to seek the blessing of anyone whose approval is a betrayal of my own values. Throughout my life, I've often been criticized by both the left and the right because I wasn't serving either interest, nor was I trying to. *The Village Voice* could just as easily attack me as the *New York Post*; I challenged both sides and refused to play by the rules of the so-called establishment. I don't need a political group or the status quo to empower me. My liberation and my empowerment are my own.

OLD-SCHOOL VERSUS NEW-SCHOOL AND BEING WOKE

In 2011, I got a call from Russell Simmons, who told me about Occupy Wall Street, the movement started in Zuccotti Park in New York City's Financial District to protest economic inequality. At the time, there weren't a lot of Black protesters involved despite the fact that the protest had been going on for about four weeks. I arrived at Zuccotti Park to meet Russell, who brought Kanye West with him, and we broadcast my radio show live from the protest that day. While we were doing that show, a group of white protesters approached me. We got into a conversation, and they explained to me that they didn't believe in a structured-leadership protest model like that of the civil rights organizations. Instead, they believed in the strategy of collectivism and rejected the model of having a charismatic leader. I told them that their goals and strategy were admirable and that they should do whatever best fit their movement. I also explained that the civil rights movement largely came out of the Black church where there was already a built-in structure and charismatic leadership at the helm. That was a model that best fit our needs.

I agreed with the core message of their protest and am in favor of the redistribution of the wealth. My so-called old-school style of protest didn't have to match theirs because we were both in favor of the same thing. There's no need to argue or debate different styles of leadership when we can be stronger together under the umbrella of a coalition. One group can favor a form of collectivism while another group may mobilize under the power of one leader. We can all sit at the same table to discuss our shared objectives. That said, it's wise to compare notes; the old school and the new school should be in dialogue with one another. A particular tactic that works for one community group may also serve someone else and vice versa. If there's one thing I've learned in the decades I've been working as an activist, it's that it's good to add new tools to the toolbox.

About ten years ago, I ran into an old acquaintance, a businessman from Chicago, who told me he was in town with MJ, *MJ* being Michael Jordan. My friend asked if I was still a member at the Havana Club and, if so, could he and MJ drop by for a cigar some time. I said sure, not expecting the meeting to happen. To my surprise, we made plans to meet later that evening. We ended up talking until about two in the morning; the club stayed open to let us do so. It's not every day that one of the world's greatest basketball players stops by. MJ's eyes kept drifting to the television screen, which was broadcasting a high-school game. I nodded at the young player who caught MJ's attention. "This young guy I've been hearing about," I said, "he any good?" MJ said, "This kid's the real deal. He's gonna be big." That ballplayer was LeBron James.

Only someone who's achieved certain success in their field can see the qualities in the next generation that will catapult them to real standing. I see this in my world of activism, too, where I'm continually scouting for the next generation of leaders and organizers, agitators and tree-shakers who will move us forward. At NAN, we've created leadership classes to help young activists get the tools they need to grow and flex. Until more of them stand up, however, the progressive youth leader will continue to be a seventy-nine-year-old white male named Bernie Sanders. Can the younger generation rise up? I hope so, because hunger, desire, and ambition don't mean anything if you don't know what you're backing.

From the new school of young activists, there's a lot of talk about being *woke*. As powerful and as necessary as being woke is, it can be misinterpreted and misused, especially when the self-appointed politically correct among us use the term as a kind of purity litmus test and deem who exactly is woke and who isn't. Wokeness is only half of the battle: once you wake up in the morning, you don't just lie in bed, luxuriating in your wokeness. You wake up to get up. You wash up using the bathroom mirror so you can go out and face the world. Your wokeness must lead to some work and vice versa; otherwise, work without wokeness is pure self-indulgence. I often tell young activists today that the best thing they can do, outside of being woke, is to work inside their communities. Doing so not only helps keep them connected but also mobilizes an entire coalition of people, all of whom can stand together, arms linked, ready to carry the cause forward.

Between a Personal and Political Reckoning

My mother Ada was fond of retelling a story about me. When she was pregnant with me, a woman approached her at the Belmont Market in Brooklyn, gently touched her pregnant belly, and told her that God was going to bless her son and that he would find greatness. During my family's darkest days—when my father had abandoned us to start a new family with his stepdaughter—my mother would invoke this story of happier days, and I would let myself dream about how I was going to make my mark in the world and honor God's grace and blessing. It filled me with resolve and a sense of duty to do right by her. I have no idea whether or not this story was true, but it didn't matter. I wanted to believe it, and so I did. Even if my mother couldn't protect me from life's cruelty, she gifted me this idea of salvation, the promise that life could be better. In my preteen years, I started preaching the Old Testament story of Hannah to congregations always with my mother in mind. Hannah promises God that if she's given a son, she'll give him back to Him to do His work. True to her word, her son Samuel would go on to become a priest and a prophet. I felt that I, like Samuel, was predestined to do God's work by virtue of my mother's fortitude. In this way, my faith connected me to God, my mother, my community, life's suffering, and hope. It connects me still.

My mother suffered from dementia for the last eight years of her life before dying on March 22, 2012. That day also marked the first national rally for Trayvon Martin's death. A few weeks prior, Ben Crump, the lawyer for Trayvon's parents, Sybrina Fulton and Tracy Martin, asked to meet with me because they couldn't get national attention for the killing of their seventeen-year-old son. Trayvon had been unarmed when he was killed by George Zimmerman, the neighborhood watchman for the gated community in which Martin's relatives lived. By the time I met with Ben, Sybrina, and Tracy, Trayvon had already been buried for two weeks. The case was so hushed that I hadn't heard the name Trayvon Martin until that very meeting, and Zimmerman had not yet been charged. Within the span of a few days, we got the word out and mobilized public outrage into a national rally in Sanford, Florida, and in other cities around the country. At the same time we were planning this rally, my mother's health was deteriorating. When my stepsister called to give me an update, I knew her time was near. The night before the rally, I woke at three thirty in the morning to catch a flight to Florida. On the way to the airport, I listened to a voice mail from my sister, who told me that my mother had died. As the car sped along the highway to Newark Airport, I wrestled with the decision I had to make: I could either go home and nurse my grief, head to Alabama to be with my sister and plan my mother's funeral, or lead the Trayvon Martin march for justice.

After decades of civil rights work and activism, I can say that I'm no stranger to making difficult or unpopular decisions. I've faced many crossroads before, but this one was particularly meaningful and difficult because it was an intersection, or so it felt, of my personal life and my professional life.

I thought about what my mother would want me to do.

I knew in my heart that she would tell me to be of

service and to lead the march. When I arrived at the airport to meet my traveling colleagues, I didn't say anything about my mother's passing. If I told them, I knew they would try to persuade me to go to Alabama, but I had already made peace with my decision. By the time we landed in Florida, I alerted some of my staff to my mother's death, and they began to reach out to the appropriate channels.

In Florida, I had a meeting scheduled with the Martin family, Crump, and the local US attorney where we planned to request a federal investigation into the matter. On the basis of Florida's Stand Your Ground statute, Zimmerman had yet to be arrested. We argued that he should be prosecuted, and we wanted the Feds to be involved. As I walked into the federal building, my cell phone rang with a blocked number. I answered and heard Valerie Jarrett's familiar voice, who told me that the president wanted to speak with me. President Obama said, "Al, I'm calling to offer my condolences for your mom." He went on, telling me about how he had coped with his own mother's death and that he and Michelle were praying for me and my family. I thanked him and was deeply moved by his words. Then he asked, "Al, where are you?" He must have heard the background noise behind me.

"I'm in Florida," I said, and I explained the Martin case, the rally, and how I was helping the family.

"You're at a rally?" he asked, shocked. "Now?"

"Not yet," I said but told him I would be there later that same day. We spoke in a bit more detail, and he assured me that he would follow the case. Then he chuckled and said, "Only Al Sharpton would be at a rally today."

That night, an estimated eight thousand people attended the Sanford rally. One week later, Martin's parents, Crump, and I were called to testify at the local county board commission for public hearings on Stand Your Ground. Jesse Jackson flew in to lend his support. Immediately following the hearing, NAN board member and my dear friend Lamell McMorris hired a private jet to bring me to my mother's wake in Dothan, Alabama. Jesse Jackson, a true friend, met me in Sanford and then also accompanied me on the plane ride to Dothan. Unfortunately, by the time we arrived, the funeral home was already closed. My brother Kenny made a few calls and arranged a special viewing for me.

We drove to the funeral home, and once we arrived, I quietly knocked on the door. It was about ten o'clock at night, and I was mindful not to make too much noise. The mortician opened the door and greeted us. He took us to a private room, and Jesse Jackson walked me to my mother's casket. The irony is that my mother had brought me to Jesse Jackson when I was twelve years old. Concerned that I was falling in with a more militant and secular group of boys, my mother spoke with Reverend William Jones, who was head of the New York chapter of Martin Luther King Jr.'s organization. Jones introduced me to Jesse, and it was through him and his mentorship that I found my way into the larger circle of civil rights. It was fitting, then, that at the end of my mother's life, it was also Jesse who called me home to her. He was the link, in more ways than one, to a life outside myself.

About a year later, the unarmed teenager Michael Brown was fatally shot by a police officer in Ferguson,

Missouri, and I found myself, once again, attending another event to honor another boy cut down early in his life. At the gathering, Lesley McSpadden, Michael's mother, said something I've never forgotten. She'd recently read a quote by Mark Twain: "The two most important days in your life are the day you are born and the day you find out why." She said that the death of her son showed her why she'd been born: she's since dedicated herself to making an impact in the world of social justice.

I often think of that quote. Had I not gone to the rally for Trayvon, then the *why* of my being brought to Reverend Jones and Jesse Jackson and of having come under the tutelage of men like Adam Clayton Powell Jr., Bishop Frederick Douglas Washington, and other prominent leaders of the Black church and the civil rights movement would have been muddied. My mother brought me to them, the same as Hannah brought Samuel to do God's work: so I could serve. It's because of my service that I've fulfilled my faith and have been lucky enough to touch a bit of greatness here and there. My mother brought me to a God-directed movement, which gave me my life's work and made it impossible for me *not* to board the plane and attend to the Martin family.

I think of my mother much in the way I think of my ancestors buried in that unmarked field in South Carolina or of my more distant relatives, those who were forcibly held against their will at the place of no return—the slave dungeon at Ghana's Cape Coast Castle—and then sent to an unknown future in an unknown world, all at the service of white men constructing the grand American experiment. This lineage

connects us all, and in this respect, the deaths of Trayvon Martin, Michael Brown, Eric Garner, Amadou Diallo, Ahmaud Arbery, Breonna Taylor, Tony McDade,
George Floyd, and too many more to name are part
of the heritage and the fallout of a country that still
deems certain lives more valuable than others. By the
same token, I often think about my grandson. When
he's living with the legacy of our failure on the environment, on administrative rollbacks that rescind human
and civil rights, will he be able to say that I did all I
could to fight that tide? If the answer is no, then I'm
doing something wrong.

While my mother knew of some of my earlier work,
she obviously didn't know about the march for Trayvon
nor of Zimmerman's acquittal. Because of her dementia, she also didn't know that I was a candidate for the
Democratic nomination for the US presidential election in 2004 or that I'm the host of television and radio
shows. My mother didn't know I was a frequent guest
of President Obama at the White House. She hadn't
even known he was our first Black president, and so it
was especially bittersweet when I received a handwrit-
ten letter from Obama commemorating my mother's
death. In the daily routine, there are a million reasons
not to get involved. Even when you do, there's a chance
no one will notice or know, but in the sweep of history,
your family isn't going to understand why you didn't
rise up, why you traded convenience for their better-
ment. Forget the pollsters. Forget the partisan talk.
Think of the people you love. Think of the people who
give your life meaning, how you measure up to them,
and make your decisions from there.

BITTERSWEET OR SWEET, NO DEFEAT

One of the first protests I participated in was with Jesse Jackson. I was fourteen years old, and we were boycotting A&P Market, who refused to hire Black workers. Some among us thought our approach should be more militant, and rather than boycotting the stores we should burn them down. The infighting was so intense, it threatened to destroy the protest entirely or, worse, divide us into separate factions. I asked Jesse why we kept putting ourselves on the line when our own kind kept fighting with us. He said, "Young buck, if you're not willing to get out there and take incoming fire, then don't sign up to be in the army." Unfortunately, the incoming fire is sometimes from your so-called allies. I learned from Jesse that it doesn't matter—if you pick your battles wisely, you can still win the war.

Movements and organizations are never perfect; for every step forward, there are two backward and vice-versa. That doesn't mean the fight isn't worth it. Adam Clayton Powell Jr. was fond of quoting Claude McKay's famous poem "If We Must Die." Powell would draw on his cigar and in that great booming voice of his summon the rally cry: "If we must die, let it not be like hogs... / Like men we'll face the murderous, cowardly pack / Pressed to the wall, dying, but fighting back!" We are a country of protesters. We are a country of agitators. We are a country of tree-shakers. There's no other choice but to fight. Otherwise, even on your best day, you're going to be treated like a second-class citizen. Bittersweet or sweet, my friend, accept no defeat.

Epilogue

GIVE ME SOMETHING TO WORK WITH

One of the most memorable events in my life was a jazz concert I attended in 2016 on the lawn of the White House, where luminaries like Herbie Hancock, Buddy Guy, Chick Corea, and others performed. But the most emotional moment for me was when I learned that the special guest performer was Aretha Franklin. Despite knowing Aretha since I was a little boy, I've always been starstruck in her company. As I made my way to my seat, Aretha's travel assistant called over to me, saying, "Hey! You wanna see the Queen?" He brought me to a small room where Aretha was sitting with her entourage, getting her hair done. It reminded me of the countless times I had watched James Brown do the very same thing, his hair done up in curlers and everyone waiting on the quick hands of his hairdresser. Aretha turned to me and exclaimed, "Reverend Al!" We talked for a bit, and then I said, "Did you ever imagine that one day you'd be getting your hair done at the White House?" We both started laughing. "We've come a long way," she said. Moments like that at the White House under Obama felt like a homecoming or an extended family reunion. And yet behind that sense of camaraderie was also a feeling of urgency: everyone knew that the other shoe was going to drop. It was just a matter of time until it did. During her performance, the Obamas sat Aisha and me close to the stage next to Elijah Cummings and his wife. No one could have told me then that only two years later I would be delivering Aretha's eulogy, and only a year after that, Elijah would leave us, too. I will never forget that evening; it was magical and bittersweet both.

Trump always saw entertainers, especially Black entertainers, as props—things to make him money. I got a first-hand sense of that in my dealing with him and Don King, who booked boxers for Trump's Atlantic City casinos. When Aretha died, Trump famously told a group of reporters that she had worked for him on numerous occasions. I couldn't let Aretha go to God without setting the record straight. During my eulogy, I said, "When word went out that Aretha passed, Trump said, 'She used to work for me.' No, she used to perform for you. She worked for us."

When I think about Aretha, I'm reminded of the countless other good men and women who also "work for us"—the Nelson Mandelas, the Shirley Chisholms and the Bayard Rustins of the world—anyone who's a tireless champion of the human spirit. We don't have to look to great public figures, however, to find hope or inspiration. People rise every day. When my father abandoned our family, my mother didn't give up. She didn't bury her head. Instead, she became the head of the household, balancing work with raising my sister and me, waking before sunlight broke to take the subway to a job that brought little personal happiness but kept food on the table. She rose.

A biracial boy, the son of a Puerto Rican mother and a Black father, who grew up in Bedford-Stuyvesant, Brooklyn, in the 1960s faced a crossroads of his own. Either he could follow in the footsteps of his older brother, who was hardened by life on the streets, or he could keep his own counsel and focus on his education. If this boy wasn't called *half-breed* by his family friends, it was either *William Hardy's son* or *Billy Hardy's brother*. It wasn't until he went to boarding school that he learned his first name: Michael. Fast-forward twenty years, and this man, Michael Hardy, became the leading attorney for NAN and one of the most prominent civil rights attorneys in the country. He could have succumbed to a different life, but instead he broke the cycle of his family's neglect and addiction, choosing to dedicate himself to protecting and fighting for human rights. He rose.

In 1965, a group of activists organized a march for voting rights. In Selma, Alabama, they linked arms and walked silently, two by two through the city streets. They didn't shrink from the violence and hatred that awaited them on the other side of Edmund Pettus Bridge. Despite being beaten that day by a hundred and fifty Alabama state troopers, their bodies pummeled to the ground, they rose. The year 2020 marked the fifty-fifth anniversary of that seminal march across the Edmund Pettus Bridge. As usual, politicians, civil rights leaders and activists of every color and orientation assembled to commemorate the anniversary. Representative John Lewis made a surprise appearance and passionately urged voters to use the ballot box, in his words, as a "nonviolent instrument or tool to redeem the soul of America." I stood on that bridge, linked arms with Jesse Jackson and thought of Aretha's words. Yes, we'd come a long way, but there's still fight in us yet.

GET YOUR KNEE OFF OUR NECK

As it turned out, the fight would come to us.

Whenever civil rights attorney Ben Crump gets in touch with me, it's not to see how I'm doing. He calls me because he knows I can't keep a secret. After I finished writing this book, Crump called me about George Floyd's death, and NAN quickly mobilized to help bring the case to national attention. As it was, the country had already been rocked by a wave of protests, with people calling for states to be reopened despite insufficient COVID-19 testing. Some of these protesters wielded assault rifles as they demanded a return to normalcy. The second wave of protests following George's death were something else entirely.

When I heard that among George's last words were "I can't breathe" as he also called for his mama, I thought of Eric Garner. How many other unknown Black men in this country have died in police custody with a choke hold or a knee pinned to their neck? It nearly broke my heart when I learned that George's mama had only recently died herself, and yet George still called out for her with his dying breath. I thought of my mother and of all the other women in our community who have been the breath for Black men for so many generations.

I asked Eric Garner's mom, Gwen Carr, if she would come to Minneapolis with me to hold vigil in George's name. She said, "Rev, I'm already packing." In Minneapolis, we visited the site where George died. I won't lie—it got to me. The reason why it affected me so much is because George's story is our story. It's the running narrative of Black folks' lives from the day we were first dragged to the shores of this country some four hundred years ago. I said as much in the first eulogy I delivered at George's memorial. The reason why Black folk could never be who we wanted to be, the reason why so many of our dreams have historically gone unfulfilled, is because you kept your knee on our neck. We were smarter than the underfunded schools you put us in, but you kept your knee on our neck. We could run corporations and not hustle in the street, but you kept your knee on our neck. We could do anything you could do, but you kept your knee on our neck. What happened to George is the same thing that happens every day in this country to Black men and women in education, health services, politics and every area of American life. We are tired of racism, discrimination, and white privilege. We are tired of the police brutality. We are tired of having your knee on our neck.

By the end of my first visit to Minneapolis, a new kind of protest had taken hold across the country. Peaceful protesters called for justice and an end to systemic racism and police brutality. These protesters demanded nothing short of equal protection under the law—a new kind of normal. Their cries that Black Lives Matter were often met by a retaliatory, militarized police force, whose violent use of batons, rubber bullets, and gas were encouraged by President Trump, a man who took shelter in the White House bunker and erected fencing to keep the protesters at bay. Around the world, people rose in protest. I knew these protests were different from Ferguson and from those in 1968 when I saw a group of Englishmen and -women tear down a statue of the seventeenth-century slave trader Edward Colston and throw it into a local river. Around the world, people are casting off the legacy of slave masters. While I've been encouraged by the show of global solidarity, especially among white folk, without real legisla-

tive change, this history-making moment risks being meaningful in symbol only. We cannot let that happen.

As a Black preacher, it's a sad fact that I attend more funer-
als than baptisms. With three memorials—in Minneapolis,
Minnesota; Raeford, North Carolina; and Houston, Texas—
George had more eulogies than most. On June 4, 2020, with
the world watching, I delivered George's last eulogy, knowing
that, after this final ceremony, there would be no more opportunities for the family to say goodbye. In time, the cameras would leave, and the family would be alone with their
grief, but not before Philonise, George's brother, would testify
before Congress, a terrible weight to carry the day after your
brother is buried. But look: I am not a fair-weather friend.
I'm the guy you call when your house has been knocked over
in a hurricane and the electric's gone. I'm the guy who will
stay by your side until the light's been restored. Just as we've
done for the families of Eric Garner, Michael Brown and others, NAN walks every step of the way on these families' long
march to justice. That Thursday afternoon, though, I con-
centrated on preparing the family to march their brother to
his grave, where he would be buried next to his mother. In
death, mother and son would be reunited, their breath given
back by God, who had first breathed life into them.

At the sermon, I said that God always uses unlikely people
to do His will. If George had been an Ivy school graduate or
someone with an impressive job title, we'd have been accused
of reacting to the loss of his prominence. If he'd been a multi-
millionaire, we'd have been accused of reacting to the unfair
loss of his wealth. If he'd been a celebrated athlete, as he was
once on a trajectory to becoming, we'd have been accused
of mourning the loss of his fame. In His good grace, though,
God took an ordinary brother from the Third Ward housing
projects, a man who nobody thought much of except those

who did know him and love him, and held him up for all to see. George was a stone that the builder rejected. All his life, he'd been rejected from jobs, athletic teams, and other opportunities. But God took that rejected stone and made him the cornerstone of a movement that's going to change the world.

After the ceremony, we made our way to the cemetery in a long procession of cars. Alongside the road were rows of mourners lined up miles long. George had been an ordinary man and yet you'd never know it from the crowds gathered to say goodbye. He could have been a president or a dignitary. Philonise turned to me and said he liked the part of the sermon when I talked about George being a rejected stone. Knowing I give all my sermons on the fly, he asked, "How did you come up with that?" I told him the truth. I said, "Because I'm a rejected stone myself." I thought of the pebbles that marked the tombstones of my ancestors. For too long, America has treated the Black family as pebbles in the dirt.

THE LIONS AND THE LAMBS

I've learned a few things in doing so many eulogies, and these hard-learned lessons seem especially meaningful during a time of so much civil unrest compounded by the deaths and global suffering caused by the Coronavirus. President Trump has yet to offer sincerely meaningful words of condolences or grace to the Floyd family. In fact, Philonise has said that the president didn't seem interested in listening to the family at all on their call with him, a startling contrast to the family's separate conversations with Joe Biden and Barack Obama, both of whom didn't hold back their support. The grief of the Floyd family echoes the pain of so many other families in America right now who have either seen the circumstances of their lives and their livelihoods cut short from systemic racism, the pandemic or, in too many instances, both. Trump has yet to nationally mourn the large-scale pain of our country.

Months before I delivered George's final eulogy, I spoke to Reverend Adolphus Lacey of Bethany Baptist Church, who was struggling to find comforting words for congregants whose family members had died from the Coronavirus. He asked me for advice. I told him the same thing I told those who gathered for Floyd's funeral service: I recalled 9/11 and how on that day I'd been campaigning for Freddy Ferrer in Brooklyn. Once I knew a second plane had hit the World Trade Center, I left our informal headquarters at Junior's Restaurant and walked to NAN in Harlem, where I faced a large group of panicked people. I searched my mind for the right words to soothe my brothers and sisters. I remembered something a friend had told me about a book he was reading. It was so good, he said, he couldn't put it down. Reading for hours and wanting sleep, he decided to cheat and skip to the end.

My advice to Reverend Lacey was this: skip to the end.

At the end of the Book of Revelations, it is promised that the first will be last and the last will be first and that "the wolf also shall dwell with the lamb, and the leopard shall lie down with the kid; and the calf and the young lion and the fatling together; and a little child shall lead them." When I face disaster like 9/11 or Coronavirus or the death of a man like George Floyd, my faith compels me to believe that the lions and the lambs will lie down together, and that God will take care of His children.

I grieve for any family who has had to let go of someone near and dear to them, but I also train my sights on those left behind. At the end of our lives, what sense does any of it make if we didn't stand for something? If we knew something wasn't right but failed to act? I tell everyone that the hardest job of being a preacher is to eulogize the life of someone who did nothing. My friends, it is harder still to eulogize the lifeblood of a country who did nothing, who sat idly by while their fellow citizens reeled in pain and could not draw a breath because of the suffocating wickedness and venom that courses through this country's veins.

For those of us fortunate enough who can join the movement calling for justice, I say, thank God for another day, a day that we neither earned nor deserved. But what are we going to do with this gift? We who are here are blessed. We who are blessed to be able to rise, because who are we if not our deeds? And so I beg of you: give me something to work with. When your time comes and I'm standing before your family as they prepare to take you to God, let there be something worthy, something of merit that you did for your fellow man that helped to lift them.

At the beginning of this book, I mentioned the refrain I most often hear from the Black community: nothing's going to change. If you look over the course of our nation's history, there's been a tremendous amount of change, most of it positive. Their glum assessment may be a frustrated response, in part, to the question I most often hear from the white community: Why is everything about race? The space between that question and the assessment made by my brothers and sisters may be vast, but it isn't impossible to bridge. The only way for us as a society—the whole of which is far greater than the sum of its parts—to mitigate that gap as well as the other inequalities of this unprecedented time is to continue to call out the wickedness in high places for what it is and to demand nothing less than a full accounting of such unfairness. George's death wasn't a tragedy. It was a crime. His death represented a common American criminal justice malfunction committed all too often on Black folk. If you violate the law, it doesn't matter if you wear blue jeans or a blue uniform, you must pay for the crime you commit.

We are a nation of change makers. If I walk over to you and knock you off your chair, that's on me. But if I come back next week and you're still on the floor, that's on you. Even if you're not responsible for going down, you're responsible for getting up. So, what are you going to do? Are you going to hide in the dark, or are you going to get up, stand on your own two feet and help direct this country toward a path of moral integrity? I think you know where I'll be. As I write this, I'm helping to plan a march on Washington, marking the anniversary of Martin Luther King Jr.'s "I Have a Dream" speech, on August 28, 2020. We are going to collect on the debt America owes us and we're going to do it in the tradition of Martin Luther King Jr., with fortitude, strength and peaceful tactics. Make no mistake, peace does not equal silence. Even when my body is laid to rest six feet under, my lips may be quiet, but my spirit will still be chanting, "No justice, no peace!"

★ ★ ★ ★ ★

Acknowledgments

It's been a journey. Let me acknowledge a few people who played major roles over the past decade in helping me see the contrasting paths of the Obama administration and the Trump administration, which led me to examine our nation at the crossroads more closely. Their insight and our subsequent conversations became the backbone of this book.

First, let me acknowledge my daughters, Dominique and Ashley, both of whom have become activists and leaders in their own right against my advice. I feared that the job of activism was so perilous that neither their mother, Kathy, nor I wanted them to be involved. Kathy has been active in the building of the National Action Network, and both Dominique and Ashley have been invaluable additions to my work and to the growth of the National Action Network.

Let me also acknowledge Aisha McShaw, my companion, girlfriend, adviser, and a constant source of support. Her enduring support is backed by her daughter, Laila Kelly, who keeps us both on our toes and updated on all the latest trends.

I want to thank my best friend through the whole journey, Dwight McKee, who's seen everything and has helped guide me through it all.

I must acknowledge Reverend W. Franklyn Richardson, a preeminent faith leader, pastor, and social activist, who chairs the board of the National Action Network.

And one of our central board members, Tanya Lombard, a giant in the corporate world.

And Jennifer Jones-Austin, who aside from being a leader in her own right of high regard and an invaluable part of our board, is also the daughter of Dr. William Augustus Jones, my pastor since the age of twelve, a man who mentored me and taught me the King tradition of civil rights activism. Jennifer continues to help carry that torch.

A special thanks to the over thirty board members of National Action Network, who gave me their full support and provided the community with a platform to put our thoughts and policies in action in the tradition of the King movement.

Let me thank Phil Griffin, Yvette Miley, and the entire management team at MSNBC and NBC for understanding my work habits and thoughts and for supporting me over the past eight years while working on *PoliticsNation with Al Sharpton*.

Thank you to all of my colleagues at MSNBC, starting with my little sister Joy-Ann Reid, who is dear to me, and to all the other hosts, including Joe Scarborough, Mika Brzezinski, and Nicole Wallace, who have never hesitated, even though they started on the other side of the aisle, to help me find ways to talk about our common ground, something that has both grown and matured my sense of activism.

And to the staff and senior producers of *PoliticsNation with Al Sharpton*, who make the show happen—thank you.

Also, let me acknowledge Alfred Liggins, CEO of Urban

One, who has, for the past fifteen years, given me a syndicated radio show to reach all major cities in Black America and been unbending in his support and his commitment in standing up for Black political and cultural independence. He has been a true brother in every sense of the word.

I would also like to thank the team of *Keepin' It Real with Rev. Al Sharpton*, headed by Fatiyn Muhammad, and a special thanks to all the stations that broadcast it live six days a week.

And I want to thank my colleagues in the civil rights movement, all of whom worked together and supported each other during the Obama years into the Trump years: Marc Morial, president, National Urban League; Derrick Johnson, president, NAACP; Sherrilyn Ifill, president and director-counsel, National Association for the Advancement of Colored People's Legal Defense and Educational Fund; Melanie Campbell, president and CEO, National Coalition on Black Civic Participation, and convener, Black Women's Roundtable Public Policy Network; Kristen Clarke, president and executive director, National Lawyers' Committee for Civil Rights Under Law; and Vanita Gupta, president and CEO, the Leadership Conference on Civil and Human Rights.

Let me thank Signe Bergstrom for her invaluable help in shaping this manuscript. And a special thanks to Peter Joseph at HarperCollins as well as to my agent, Josh Getzler. A heartfelt and sincere thanks to the inimitable Dr. Michael Eric Dyson, a man who says it better than I could myself.

Last but not least, let me thank the members, staff, and chapter leaders of the National Action Network, who are now in 106 cities under the coordination of our national field director, Reverend DeVes Toon. And to our staff of almost fifty people, who get up every day and do hard, underappreciated work in our six regional offices nationwide. Without them, it would be impossible to confront and deal with many of the injustices and the unfairness this book addresses. People see me out front but they are the real heroes—the coalition that not only makes me "me," but that has also kept the movement alive and true to the spirit of the King tradition.

Bibliography

Aldred, Jessica, and Lauren Goodchild. "Timeline: Al Gore." *The Guardian*. October 12, 2007. https://www.theguardian.com/environment/2007/oct/12/climatechange1.

Andrews, Suzanna. "Everything Al Sharpton Has Lived for Is at Stake This November." *Vanity Fair*. April 2016. https://www.vanityfair.com/news/2016/03/al-sharpton-civil-rights-politics.

Associated Press. "Newsom Grants Posthumous Pardon to Bayard Rustin, Civil Rights Leader Arrested on 'Morals Charge.'" KTLA. Updated February 5, 2020. https://ktla.com/news/local-news/newsom-grants-posthumous-pardon-to-bayard-rustin-civil-rights-leader-arrested-on-morals-charge/.

———. "Thurmond's Daughter: Sharpton 'Overreacted.'" NBCNews.com. Updated February 27, 2007. http://www.nbcnews.com/id/17326922/ns/us_news-life/t/thurmonds-daughter-sharpton-overreacted/#.XmfLCkMpCi4.

———. "A Timeline of the Water Crisis in Flint, Michigan." AP News. June 14, 2017. https://apnews.com/1176657a4b0d468c8f35ddbb07f12bec.

Averbuch, Maya, and Kirk Semple. "Migrant Caravan Continues North, Defying Mexico and U.S." *New York Times*. October 20, 2018. https://www.nytimes.com/2018/10/20/world/americas/migrants-caravan-mexico.html.

Ball, Molly. "Donald Trump Didn't Really Win 52% of White Women in 2016." *Time*. October 18, 2018. https://time.com/5422644/trump-white-women-2016/.

Batalova, Jeanne, Brittany Blizzard, and Jessica Bolter. "Frequently Requested Statistics on Immigrants and Immigration in the United States." Migration Policy Institute. February 14, 2020. https://www.migrationpolicy.org/article/frequently-requested-statistics-immigrants-and-immigration-united-states.

Bellafante, Ginia. "Resurrecting Brownsville." *The Nation*. April 17, 2013. https://www.thenation.com/article/archive/resurrecting-brownsville/.

Berry, Daina Ramey, and Kali Nicole Gross. *A Black Women's History of the United States*. Boston: Beacon Press, 2020.

Berry, Mary Frances. *History Teaches Us to Resist: How Progressive Movements Have Succeeded in Challenging Times*. Boston: Beacon Press, 2018.

Brenner, Marie. "How Donald Trump and Roy Cohn's Ruthless Symbiosis Changed America." *Vanity Fair*. June 28, 2017. https://www.vanityfair.com/news/2017/06/donald-trump-roy-cohn-relationship.

Brockell, Gillian. "The Transgender Women at Stonewall Were Pushed Out of the Gay Rights Movement. Now They Are Getting a Statue in New York." *Washington Post*. July 12, 2019. https://www.washingtonpost.com/history/2019/06/12/transgender-women-heart-stonewall-riots-are-getting-statue-new-york/.

Buchanan, Larry, Jugal K. Patel, Brian M. Rosenthal, and Anjali Singhvi. "A Month of Coronavirus in New York City: See the Hardest-Hit Areas." *New York Times*. April 1, 2020. https://www.nytimes.

com/interactive/2020/04/01/nyregion/nyc-coronavirus-cases-map.
html?action=click&module=Top%20Stories&pgtype=Homepage.

Budhos, Marina. "Donald Trump's Childhood in Queens Can Explain His Obsession with Borders." *Quartz*. October 20, 2016. https://
qz.com/814851/donald-trumps-childhood-in-queens-can-explain-his-
obsession-with-borders/.

Bump, Philip. "Want to Know Where Most Drugs Cross the Border?
Look at the Border Patrol's News Releases." *Washington Post*. February
1, 2019. https://www.washingtonpost.com/politics/2019/02/01/want-
know-where-most-drugs-cross-border-look-border-patrols-press-
releases/.

Carlson, Tucker. "The League of Extraordinary Gentlemen." *Esquire*.
July 14, 2009. https://www.esquire.com/news-politics/a450/esq1103-
nov-liberia-rev/.

———. "Mitt Romney Supports the Status Quo. But for Everyone
Else, It's Infuriating." Fox News. Published January 3, 2019. Mono-
logue. YouTube video, 15:13. https://www.foxnews.com/opinion/
tucker-carlson-mitt-romney-supports-the-status-quo-but-for-everyone-
else-its-infuriating.

Carrington, Damian. "Earth's Sixth Mass Extinction Event Under Way,
Scientists Warn." *The Guardian*. July 10, 2017. https://www.theguard-
ian.com/environment/2017/jul/10/earths-sixth-mass-extinction-event-
already-underway-scientists-warn.

Cascone, Sarah. "The Unused Confetti From Hillary Clinton's Elec-
tion-Night Loss Is Now a Work of Art." *Artnet News*. July 6, 2017.
https://news.artnet.com/art-world/bunny-burson-confetti-hillary-
clinton-1015193.

Chisholm, Shirley. *Unbought and Unbossed*. Boston: Houghton Mifflin
Harcourt, 1970.

Coates, Ta-Nehisi. *Between the World and Me.* New York: Spiegel & Grau, 2015.

————. "The Case for Reparations." *The Atlantic.* June 2014. https://www.theatlantic.com/magazine/archive/2014/06/the-case-for-reparations/361631/.

Corley, Cheryl. "Bayard Rustin: The Man Who Organized the March on Washington." NPR: *All Things Considered.* August 15, 2013, 7:29. https://www.npr.org/sections/codeswitch/2013/08/15/212338844/bayard-rustin-the-man-who-organized-the-march-on-washington.

Davenport, Coral. "U.S. to Announce Rollback of Auto Pollution Rules, a Key Effort to Fight Climate Change." *New York Times.* Updated March 31, 2020. https://www.nytimes.com/2020/03/30/climate/trump-fuel-economy.html?action=click&module=Top%20Stories&pgtype=Homepage.

Dyson, Michael Eric. *Tears We Cannot Stop: A Sermon to White America.* New York: St. Martin's Press, 2017.

Edsall, Thomas B. "How Racist Is Trump's Republican Party?" *New York Times.* March 18, 2020. https://www.nytimes.com/2020/03/18/opinion/trump-republicans-racism.html.

Flagg, Anna. "Is There a Connection Between Undocumented Immigrants and Crime?" Marshall Project. May 13, 2019. https://www.themarshallproject.org/2019/05/13/is-there-a-connection-between-undocumented-immigrants-and-crime.

Foner, Eric. *The Fiery Trial: Abraham Lincoln and American Slavery.* New York: W.W. Norton, 2010.

Galli, Mark. "Trump Should Be Removed from Office." *Christianity Today.* December 19, 2019. https://www.christianitytoday.com/ct/2019/december-web-only/trump-should-be-removed-from-office.html.

Graham, David A. "Are Children Being Kept in 'Cages' at the Border?"

The Atlantic. June 18, 2018. https://www.theatlantic.com/politics/archive/2018/06/ceci-nest-pas-une-cage/563072/.

Hale, Kori. "The Economic Impact of COVID-19 Will Hit Minorities the Hardest." *Forbes*. March 17, 2020. https://www.forbes.com/sites/korihale/2020/03/17/the-economic-impact-of-covid-19-will-hit-minorities-the-hardest/#110c23d010c0.

History.com Eds. "The Great Migration." History. Updated January 16, 2020. https://www.history.com/topics/black-history/great-migration.

Huang, Jon, Samuel Jacoby, Michael Strickland, and K.K. Rebecca Lai. "Election 2016: Exit Polls." *New York Times*. November 8, 2016. https://www.nytimes.com/interactive/2016/11/08/us/politics/election-exit-polls.html.

Human Rights Campaign. "Being African American & LGBTQ: An Introduction." April 10, 2020. https://www.hrc.org/resources/being-african-american-lgbtq-an-introduction.

Isidore, Chris. "Black Unemployment Rate Falls to a Record Low." CNN Business. Updated September 6, 2019. https://www.cnn.com/2019/09/06/economy/black-unemployment-rate/index.html.

Jacobs, Julia. "Sessions's Use of Bible Passage to Defend Immigration Policy Draws Fire." *New York Times*. June 15, 2018. https://www.nytimes.com/2018/06/15/us/sessions-bible-verse-romans.html.

Jordan, Miriam. "'We're Petrified': Immigrants Afraid to Seek Medical Care for Coronavirus." *New York Times*. Updated April 10, 2020. https://www.nytimes.com/2020/03/18/us/coronavirus-immigrants.html.

Joung, Madeleine. "What Is Happening at Migrant Detention Centers? Here's What to Know." *Time*. Updated July 12, 2019. https://time.com/5623148/migrant-detention-centers-conditions/.

Kazin, Michael. "How Labor Learned to Love Immigration." *New Re-*

public. May 13, 2013. https://newrepublic.com/article/113203/labor-and-immigration-how-unions-got-board-immigration-reform.

King, Jamilah. "Meet the Trans Women of Color Who Helped Put Stonewall on the Map." *Mic.* June 25, 2015. https://www.mic.com/articles/121256/meet-marsha-p-johnson-and-sylvia-rivera-transgender-stonewall-veterans.

Klein, Ezra. "Why Democrats Still Have to Appeal to the Center, but Republicans Don't." *New York Times.* January 24, 2020. https://www.nytimes.com/2020/01/24/opinion/sunday/democrats-republicans-polarization.html?searchResultPosition=2.

Klein, Naomi. *On Fire: The (Burning) Case for a Green New Deal.* New York: Simon & Schuster, 2019.

Koren, Marina. "The Pandemic Is Turning the Natural World Upside Down." *The Atlantic.* April 2, 2020. https://www.theatlantic.com/science/archive/2020/04/coronavirus-pandemic-earth-pollution-noise/609316/.

Krugman, Paul. "Trump the Intimidator Fails Again." *New York Times.* January 6, 2020. https://www.nytimes.com/2020/01/06/opinion/trump-iran-trade.html?searchResultPosition=9.

Kurtzleben, Danielle, Sean McMinn, and Renee Klahr. "What It Looks Like to Have a Record Number of Women in the House of Representatives." NPR. January 4, 2019. https://www.npr.org/2019/01/04/678227272/what-it-looks-like-to-have-a-record-number-of-women-in-the-house-of-representati.

Leadership Conference on Civil & Human Rights. "Trump Administration Civil and Human Rights Rollbacks." March 18, 2020. https://civilrights.org/trump-rollbacks/.

Leininger, Alex. "Hundreds Flock to Susan B. Anthony's Grave on Election Day." CNN. Updated November 8, 2016. https://www.cnn.com/2016/11/08/politics/susan-b-anthony-gravesite-voting-stickers-irpt/index.html.

Lepore, Jill. *These Truths: A History of the United States.* New York: W.W. Norton, 2018.

Liesman, Steve. "Majority of Americans Support Progressive Policies Such as Higher Minimum Wage, Free College." CNBC (website). Updated March 27, 2019. https://www.cnbc.com/2019/03/27/majority-of-americans-support-progressive-policies-such-as-paid-maternity-leave-free-college.html.

"Listen to Newly Released Recordings of Trump Pretending to Be 'John Barron' in 1980s Phone Interviews." Digg (website). Updated June 26, 2019. https://digg.com/2018/trump-john-barron-recordings.

Lockheart, P.R. "Trump Says He Deserves Credit for the Lowest Black Unemployment Rate in Decates. He Doesn't." *Vox.* Updated January 30, 2018. https://www.vox.com/policy-and-politics/2018/1/18/16902390/trump-black-unemployment-rate-record-decline.

Lowery, Wesley. *"They Can't Kill Us All": Ferguson, Baltimore, and a New Era in America's Racial Justice Movement.* New York: Little, Brown, 2016.

Martin, Michel, and Emma Bowman. "In Newly Found Audio, a Forgotten Civil Rights Leader Says Coming Out 'Was an Absolute Necessity.'" NPR: *All Things Considered.* January 6, 2019, 9:00. https://www.npr.org/2019/01/06/682598649/in-newly-found-audio-a-forgotten-civil-rights-leader-says-coming-out-was-an-abso.

Martínez, Jessica, and Gregory A. Smith. "How the Faithful Voted: A Preliminary 2016 Analysis." Pew Research Center. November 9, 2016. https://www.pewresearch.org/fact-tank/2016/11/09/how-the-faithful-voted-a-preliminary-2016-analysis/.

Mena, Kelly. "Appeals Court Sides with Florida Ex-Felons in Fight for Voting Rights." CNN. February 19, 2020. https://www.cnn.com/2020/02/19/politics/florida-court-upholds-felons-right-to-vote/index.html.

Nonko, Emily. "Redlining: How One Racist, Depression-Era Policy

Still Shapes New York Real Estate." *Brick Underground*. December 29, 2016. https://www.brickunderground.com/blog/2015/10/history_of_redlining.

Obama, Barack. *The Audacity of Hope: Thoughts on Reclaiming the American Dream*. New York: Three Rivers Press, 2006.

———. "The Nelson Mandela Lecture." *New Yorker*. July 19, 2018. https://www.newyorker.com/news/news-desk/the-nelson-mandela-lecture-barack-obama-johannesburg.

O'Hara, Mary Emily. "Trump Pulls Back Obama-Era Protections for Women Workers." NBC News. Updated April 3, 2017. https://www.nbcnews.com/news/us-news/trump-pulls-back-obama-era-protections-women-workers-n741041.

Ousey, Graham C., and Charis E. Kubrin. "Immigration and Crime: Assessing a Contentious Issue." *Annual Review of Criminology* 1 (2018): 63–84. https://www.annualreviews.org/doi/pdf/10.1146/annurev-criminol-032317-092026.

Pengelly, Martin. "Georgetown Students Vote to Pay Reparations for Slaves Sold by University." *The Guardian*. April 15, 2019. https://www.theguardian.com/world/2019/apr/15/georgetown-students-reparations-vote-slaves-sold-by-university.

Pew Research Center. "An Examination of the 2016 Electorate, Based on Validated Voters" in *For Most Trump Voters, "Very Warm" Feelings for Him Endured*. August 9, 2018. https://www.people-press.org/2018/08/09/an-examination-of-the-2016-electorate-based-on-validated-voters/.

———. "Attitudes on Same-Sex Marriage." Pew Research Center. May 14, 2019. https://www.pewforum.org/fact-sheet/changing-attitudes-on-gay-marriage/.

Pierre-Louis, Kendra. "A Leader in the War on Poverty Opens a New Front: Pollution." *New York Times*. August 24, 2018. https://www.nytimes.com/2018/08/24/climate/coal-ash-pollution-poverty.html.

Planas, Roque, and Ryan Grim. "Here's How the U.S. Sparked a Refugee Crisis on the Border, in 8 Simple Steps." *Huffpost*. Updated November 5, 2014. https://www.huffpost.com/entry/refugee-crisis-border_n_5596125.

Reuters. "Trayvon Martin Rally in Florida Calls for Neighborhood Watchman Arrest." *The Guardian*. March 23, 2012. Video:1:58. https://www.theguardian.com/world/video/2012/mar/23/trayvon-martin-florida-sanford-rally.

Rothman, Lily. "Donald Trump's 1973 Discrimination Case Really Was Part of Something Larger." *Time*. September 28, 2016. https://time.com/4508889/presidential-debate-1970s-bias-donald-trump/.

Ruiz, Rebecca R., Robert Gebeloff, Steve Eder, and Ben Protess. "A Conservative Agenda Unleashed on the Federal Courts." *New York Times*. Updated March 16, 2020. https://www.nytimes.com/2020/03/14/us/trump-appeals-court-judges.html.

Scott, Eugene. "Before the Midterms, Trump Harped on the Migrant Caravan. Since Then, He Hasn't Brought It Up." *Washington Post*. November 8, 2018. https://www.washingtonpost.com/politics/2018/11/08/before-midterms-trump-harped-migrant-caravan-since-then-he-has-barely-mentioned-it/.

Sisson, Patrick. "How Trump Is Rolling Back Housing Desegregation Rules, Explained." *Curbed* (blog). January 28, 2020. https://www.curbed.com/2020/1/28/21101127/trump-hud-housing-segregation-ben-carson.

Skelton, Renee, and Vernice Miller. "The Environmental Justice Movement." Natural Resources Defense Council. March 17, 2016. https://www.nrdc.org/stories/environmental-justice-movement.

Slattery, Denis, and Chauncey Alcorn. "Time for Action Against 'Immoral' Detention of Children at Border, Sharpton Says." *NY Daily News*. June 16, 2018. https://www.nydailynews.com/new-york/ny-metro-sharpton-sessions-border-20180616-story.html.

Smith, Mitch, Julie Bosman, and Monica Davey. "Flint's Water Crisis Started 5 Years Ago. It's Not Over." *New York Times*. April 25, 2019. https://www.nytimes.com/2019/04/25/us/flint-water-crisis.html.

Stodghill, Alexis Garrett. "President Obama and First Family Attend Services at Oldest Black Episcopal Church." *The Grio*. January 20, 2013. https://thegrio.com/2013/01/20/president-obama-and-first-family-attend-services-at-oldest-black-episcopal-church/.

Tauer, Kristen. "Robert De Niro, Harvey Weinstein Throw Election Night Party." *WWD*. November 9, 2016. https://wwd.com/eye/parties/robert-de-niro-harvey-weinstein-jay-penske-election-night-party-10702116/.

Tavernise, Sabrina, and Robert Gebeloff. "How Voters Turned Virginia from Deep Red to Solid Blue." *New York Times*. November 9, 2019. https://www.nytimes.com/2019/11/09/us/virginia-elections-democrats-republicans.html.

Tesfaye, Sophia. "'I Say Nothing': Birther Godfather Donald Trump Declines to Apologize to African-Americans, Obama in First Debate." *Salon*. September 27, 2016. https://www.salon.com/test/2016/09/27/i-say-nothing-trump-refuses-to-apologize-to-african-americans-and-president-obama-for-his-birtherism-during-first-debate/.

Trump, Donald. "I'm Sorry, by Donald Trump." Compiled by Sue Horton. *Los Angeles Times*. August 18, 2019. https://www.latimes.com/opinion/story/2019-08-16/president-trump-twitter-apologize-sorry.

———. Trump Twitter Archive. Website created by Brendan Brown. March 9, 2020. http://trumptwitterarchive.com/archive.

Ware, Susan. *Why They Marched: Untold Stories of the Women Who Fought for the Right to Vote*. March 9, 2020. Cambridge, MA: Belknap Press of Harvard University Press, 2019.

Warren, Elizabeth. "Elizabeth Warren Announces She Is Ending Her Presidential Campaign." CBS News. Streamed live on March 5, 2020. You-Tube video, 8:37. https://www.youtube.com/watch?v=e6dkUWAObzA.

Watson, Walter Ray. "A Look Back on Shirley Chisholm's Historic 1968 House Victory." NPR: *Morning Edition*. Updated November 16, 2018, 3:31. https://www.npr.org/2018/11/06/664617076/a-look-back-on-shirley-chisholm-s-historic-1968-house-victory.

Wesleyan University. "Black Women & the Suffrage Movement: 1848–1923." Excerpts taken from *One of Divided Sisters: Bridging the Gap Between Black and White Women* by Midge Wilson and Kathy Russell. New York: Anchor, 1996 and PBS.org. https://www.wesleyan.edu/mlk/posters/suffrage.html.

Wolf, Richard. "Supreme Court Blocks 2020 Census Citizenship Question for Now, Handing Trump Administration a Major Defeat." *USA TODAY*. Updated June 27, 2019. https://www.usatoday.com/story/news/politics/2019/06/27/2020-census-citizenship-question-supreme-court-avoids-trump-request/1289738001/.

Wolf, Richard, and Brad Heath. "Supreme Court Strikes Down Key Part of Voting Rights Act." *USA TODAY*. Updated June 25, 2013. https://www.usatoday.com/story/news/politics/2013/06/25/supreme-court-shelby-voting-rights-alabama-congress-race/2116491/.

World Bank (website). "GDP, PPP (Constant 2011 International $)—Russian Federation, China, United States." World Bank, International Comparison Program database. April 1, 2020. https://data.worldbank.org/indicator/NY.GDP.MKTP.PP.KD?locations=RU-CN-US.

Wren, Adam. "What Mayor Pete Couldn't Fix About the South Bend Cops." *Politico Magazine*. June 22, 2019. https://www.politico.com/magazine/story/2019/06/22/pete-buttigieg-police-shooting-227206.